Seeing Yourself See

Seeing Yourself See

Eye Exercises for Total Vision

By Jim Jackson

Original illustrations and photographs by the author

Saturday Review Press / E. P. Dutton & Co., Inc.
/ New York

Copyright © 1975 by Jim Jackson
All rights reserved. Printed in the U.S.A.
First Edition
10 9 8 7 6 5 4 3 2 1

Published simultaneously in Canada by
Clarke, Irwin & Company Limited, Toronto and Vancouver
ISBN: 0-8415-0401-6 (cloth)   0-8415-0402-4 (paper)

Library of Congress Cataloging in Publication Data

Jackson, Jim.
   Seeing yourself see.

   Bibliography: p.
   1. Visual perception.   2. Visual discrimination.
I. Title.
QP475.5.J3 1975   152.1′4   75-11810

To Leslie Corin

My sincere love and gratitude to Leslie Corin for the time she spent helping prepare this book. Also, I owe a great debt to Toinette L. E. Rees for continually pushing me to write and rewrite. Without the persistent encouragement and editorial advice of these two women, this book would still be a few rough sketches and some cursory descriptions tucked in the back of my portfolio.

Thanks to all those friends who offered suggestions and supported my work with their enthusiasm.

Contents

Introduction   13

1. The Framework of Seeing   15
A description of the built-in visual structure that surrounds everything your eyes see

2. Demonstrating How Your Eyes Work   32
Techniques to help you experience the workings of your field of vision, focal point, and stereoscopic ability

3. Exercising Your Sense of Seeing   61
Visual care exercises from therapists, hatha yoga, and the People's Republic of China

4. The Eye, the Mind, and Meditation   90
The role of a personal visual sense in contemplation, meditation, and creative thinking

5. Art and Visual Apperception   107
A discussion of the application of visual consciousness in art, past and present

Bibliography   125

That was a flashbulb going off in your face, and you were looking right into it. You frown and grumble because for a second you are blinded. Then, as your sight returns, you notice an annoying dark spot hovering in the center of your vision that obscures everything you look at. You blink your eyes, curse the photographer, and strain to see past the spot. For the next fifteen minutes you wish it would go away so you can see what you are doing, but you hardly notice when it slowly disappears.

It's typical of us to be unaware of our vision until our eyes give us trouble. This is unfortunate because there are many benefits to be gained from their creative use and a heightened consciousness of their function.

From my experience I've learned that achieving a sense of creative vision and perhaps even better eyesight comes through developing a personal consciousness of the process of seeing. I call the process *seeing yourself see*. The more academic term is *visual apperception*, which refers to the mind being conscious of its own visual function. Seeing yourself see is both a means of recycling visual information through the mind and a method of introspection and self-realization that can yield a better understanding of yourself and a more firmly centered sense of self.

The success of this approach will depend on the effort you are willing to make. Some people already have an ongoing concern for the function of their senses; others are curious why those flashbulb spots linger so long. Some are squeamish about learning to be aware of their eyes or any bodily function and will probably resist the exercises suggested. Nevertheless, each person willing to try, even the squeamish, can gain something of value from this process. You may discover a visual disorder early enough to have it successfully treated, or you may be able to improve your eyesight. You may see things you never knew existed, or you may find help in developing your own creative abilities. It's your ball game.

First you will be shown how to see your own eyes working; then you will be led through exercises that can help improve the function of your eyes as well as help develop techniques for mental control. Finally, to show that there are productive uses for these skills, we will discuss some of the ways visual consciousness has influenced art, past and present.

1 / The Framework of Seeing

As an artist I remember one particular figure-drawing class when the hired model didn't show up. Our instructor asked each student to model fully clothed for the others. Most of us hated this chore because of the boredom of posing and the embarrassment of being scrutinized so closely by so many for so long. When my turn came, I froze in a seated position so that I could look out the window at the trees and hills. I hoped the pleasant view would help fight the boredom.

As I scanned the landscape I remembered my plans to do some paintings that would capture the attention of viewers by repeating aspects of their own seeing. So I decided to analyze how my eyes were seeing the trees and hills, rather than just experience those images.

As I concentrated on staring out the window, I experienced an entirely new series of visual sensations. For the first time in my life, I actually saw the boundaries of my eyes creating a frame around the window which outlined the landscape. Immediately, ideas came to mind for approaching my planned paintings, along with the exciting realization that I was experiencing a completely new sensation. A hidden door had opened.

Several years later, after a number of other such experiences, I was sitting on a beach looking out at a heavy mist. It was so dense it obscured the horizon line and blended with the water, so that sky and water seemed to be one. The sky was water and the water, sky. This blue gray haze seemed to drift out and around, and slowly I became aware that it completely surrounded the span of my vision. As I gazed into the mist again, I concentrated on how my eyes were doing their seeing. Occasionally I had to blink or my eyes would burn, but I kept my eyes fixed in the center of that mist. After about five minutes, areas of blue and red, irregular in shape and lighted so that they glowed softly, faded in and out of the mist. I sensed that my eyes had probably become saturated with the misty light and were adding their own embellishments.

I was stunned by the total sensory effect. The whole environment at that moment seemed to be a special kind of creative vision suggesting colors and feelings beyond even the seashore.

I've worked for a long time trying to communicate those experiences through my paintings and drawings and, now, through this book. A primary purpose of the book is to present information about your eyes in such a way that you'll be able to have a personal visual experience within yourself— not to read and learn facts, but actually to experience the seeing part of yourself, and through that experience to understand better the fundamental nature of your being.

It's like learning to operate a TV camera. First you have to learn about lenses, wiring, cathode tubes, etc.—the matrix of the medium. You can learn about your eyes in the same way. Life without eyesight is considered to be seriously handicapped. If vision is so important, try to understand your own visual matrix.

The demonstrations, exercises, diagrams, and drawings are presented to serve as a guide through a series of experiences that will make you more conscious of the function of your eyes. I feel that the process will, in time, yield a more creative consciousness and help develop creative skills as well as improve the aesthetic quality of vision.

Some Points To Keep in Mind

Specific instructions to guide your experience are presented in **bold-face type** throughout the book so you can easily differentiate between exercises and explanations.

If you do not experience the effects described in some of the exercises on the first try, then try again slowly, perhaps at another time. Some people don't respond immediately and should avoid trying to complete the book in one session. Even though the procedure may look like child's play at first glance, the experiences can be deeply revealing.

If this material leads you to suspect that your eyes are not working well, see an eye doctor (ophthalmologist) as soon as possible. Serious eye diseases can be treated with remarkable success if diagnosed early enough.

Please don't expect too much of yourself; the exercises are not intended as standards of normality. A person with normal vision may not be able to respond to the exercises the first time. They are intended to help you develop your own insights, not to compete with me or anyone else.

If you wear glasses, try the exercises with them on and later with them off. If you have a serious visual handicap, such as sight in only one eye, try to take the handicap into account, but don't give up. You may find that you will better understand your handicap, and the exercises may help you learn to function better with what eyesight you have.

As you read on, look over the drawings and calmly consider the exercises without concern for success or failure. Make a quiet, honest effort. Turn your attention inside yourself. See yourself seeing. Be yourself being.

To Become Aware of the Framework of Seeing

We will start with seeing a shape that is hidden within your field of vision. It is the central area of a framework created by the boundaries of your eyes. You can experience that shape within yourself. Just keep the drawing below in mind as you follow the next steps.

Look down at the tip of your nose.

There will appear to be two noses because you are seeing each side of your nose simultaneously with each of your two eyes, respectively. If you close one eye, you see the side of one nose; it takes two eyes to see two noses.

The two noses will always be blurry because they are too close to the eyes to be seen clearly. So just concentrate on seeing indirectly, off to the side.

Roll your eyes around in a circle, starting at the tip of one nose and following the edge of that nose up to the eyebrows and over and down the edge of your other nose.

This movement outlines the shape of the central area of the framework. It is a fuzzy mushroom shape like the drawing.

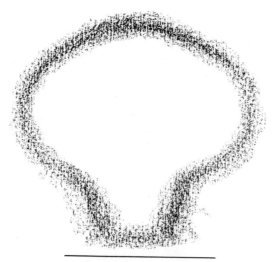

CENTRAL FRAME OF VISION.

Even though seeing two noses and the shape of the central frame seemed simple enough to me, I discovered that a number of people could not see their two noses, even when I was present to give them verbal instructions.

Because this is a basic experience for people with two functioning eyes, it is important that at some point you see two noses. You will probably have no trouble at all—most people don't. If you do have trouble, I suggest that you close one eye and look at one side of your nose with your open eye and then reverse the procedure. This can help because both eyes seldom see with equal clarity and the dominant eye will tend to see its side of the nose more clearly when both eyes are open. It also helps if you face a light so that both sides of your nose are equally lighted.

Seeing two noses leads to seeing the central frame, and this is important in the context of this book. But if you don't see them right away, continue with the other demonstrations and exercises that follow. You may have no trouble at all. Later, you can return to this demonstration at your leisure until you accomplish it.

A friend who has followed my development of this process for about two years finally saw her two noses while lying on her back looking at the ceiling during a yoga session. She was utterly amazed, and I expressed disbelief because I thought she had seen them a long time ago. She admitted she didn't have the heart to tell me.

So if it takes you a while, don't give up. If the effort makes you unpleasantly self-conscious, feel free to continue with the other exercises and keep trying at times when you are in a relaxed state of mind. Eventually, you will see two noses and you will have made an important start toward seeing yourself see.

Let's go one more step and see the two areas that are to the left and right of the central area you just experienced. You have probably often referred to the two areas as the corners of your eyes. Those corners are known as the areas of peripheral vision. There is a large area of peripheral vision in each eye, and the two eyes together in their side-by-side position create two peripheral areas seen simultaneously.

Let's try to see the total frame including the peripheral framework.

Concentrate.

Look as far to your right and left as you can without straining your eyes.

As you hold your head straight forward, you will probably be able to see your shoulders at the outer edge of your vision.

Don't strain.

The edge of your visual field will be blurred so try to accept whatever you see as a blur without trying to see it clearly.

Now look down, keeping your head still.

Slowly, roll your eyes in a circle following the outer edge of the peripheral areas up and over and down to the other edge.

Feel the eye muscles stretch, but don't strain.

As you follow that blurry edge, you will see the total frame through which you see. It has a shape similar to the drawing.

TOTAL FRAME OF VISION.

Each eye has its own frame and it can be easily seen.

Without actually touching your right eye, cover it with the palm of your cupped hand. Leave your left eye open.

Stretch your left eye around, find your nose, look up and over and down following the blurry edge, and you will see the frame of your left eye.

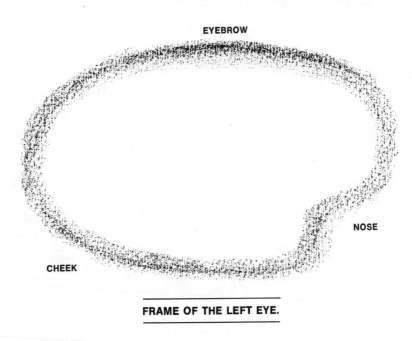

FRAME OF THE LEFT EYE.

Seeing the frame of the right eye is similar.

Cover your left eye without touching it.

As you rotate your right eye you will also see its frame.

By now it's easy to see that your eyelids, eyebrows, nose, and cheeks create the shape of each eye's framework. Your own individual features affect the shape of that framework.

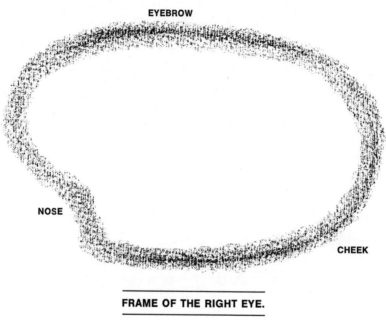

FRAME OF THE RIGHT EYE.

When you have both eyes open, the frames of the left and the right eyes mix to create the total framework.

Open both eyes.

Roll them around slowly and easily to see the total framework.

Where the two frames overlap, two noses bracket your central area of vision, and the portions off to the sides become the peripheral areas of the framework.

FRAMES OF THE TWO EYES OVERLAP.

If you try drawing some of the simple shapes you see when you begin to look at your visual framework, you will appreciate the difficulty I had devising easily visualized diagrams. So, let me explain a bit about these drawings, especially the ones that follow.

These drawings are intended to help you experience the kind of personalized seeing this book introduces. Words don't seem to be enough. So try to read the drawings with the same care you take to read the words. That way, the points my words are trying to make may seem less mysterious.

In the drawings, the framework is indistinct because we cannot depict an exact image of what we really see. Changing lighting conditions, body positions, and psychological states cause an endless variety of visual impressions of the framework, without taking into account all the possible variations created by eyelids, cheekbones, and eyebrows of different types.

THE TOTAL BEING ENCLOSING THE VISUAL SENSE.

The oval shape represents the framework and the black outline represents the darkness you see when your eye turns far enough to the side to see under the eyelid. This is the limit of the eye's movement and the limit of what it can see. In most of my drawings a rectangular frame, shaded with an even dark gray tone, surrounds the oval. It is there in an abstract way to keep you aware that vision is not a thing unto itself, but an essential part of your whole being. You can think of the gray rectangle as a symbol of all the aspects of your being that are outside your visual sense yet within the limits of your body and its other senses. The concept becomes easy to understand when you think of yourself looking out through your eyes and simultaneously keep in mind an awareness of all yourself—your total being.

When the oval is completely blacked in, it represents the blackness your eyes see when they are closed. It also serves as a rest stop. If at any time reading or doing the exercises makes your eyes sting or feel tired or strained, stop and follow these steps:

Close your eyes.

Breathe deeply.

Relax.

Enjoy the darkness.

Rest.

Imagine a large black velvet oval inside your head behind your nose and forehead.

Do not return to the material until your eyes feel perfectly restored.

The black oval is repeated throughout the book to indicate rest stops you should take, tired or not. The stops will prevent strain because your eyes need rest most just before they begin to feel tired, not after they are red and watery.

Other books don't come with rest breaks, so you will have to establish a program for reading and resting. This is the only way to avoid strain—you can't feel it coming until it's too late.

During long reading sessions, look up from the book every two or three pages and focus into the distance for a moment.

Every fifteen minutes pause and close your eyes for at least two minutes.

After two hours, stop reading for at least fifteen minutes. Rest with your eyes closed. Then stare into the distance for five minutes. (Looking out the window and daydreaming are good.)

These steps are also necessary when you are sewing, drawing, or doing other close work.

When you have a basic understanding of the visual framework, you can then begin to investigate your own particular visual frame.

You can change the shape of your visual frame just by squinting your eyelids close together,

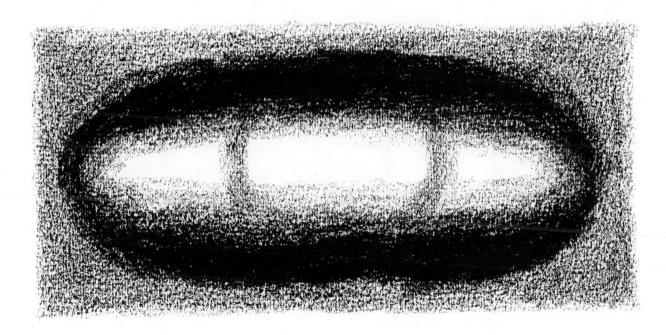

Wearing glasses,

Crossing your eyes and looking at your nose,

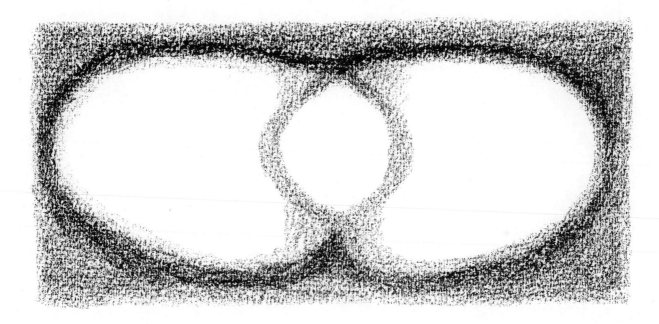

Growing long hair over your face or a bump on your nose.

You can see the wart on the left side of your nose and the light shining on it.

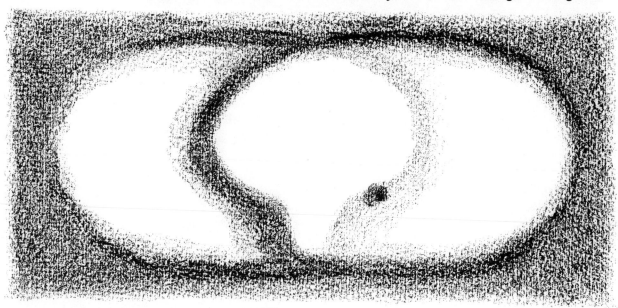

Your frame of vision is uniquely your own.

2 / Demonstrating How Your Eyes Work

You just feel it. Someone is sneaking up behind you. Without a thought, you turn. There stands your old best buddy with a toothy smile ready to give you the ol' rib jab.

How could you have known someone was coming up from behind? Perhaps it was a sixth sense or eyes in the back of your head, but more than likely, it was the outer regions of your peripheral vision detecting a suspicious movement and triggering a reflex action. This is instinctive. Your vision does more than just guide you down the sidewalk or enable you to read books.

The ball player works hours trying to develop a reflex response between his eye and his hand. He improves his ability to focus instantly on an objective and responds automatically with the proper movements so that he catches the ball, or shoots the goal, or hits the home run, or kicks the field goal.

The artist works to establish a similar reflex between the eye and the hand so that he has an automatic ability to draw what he observes.

Practicing seeing sharpens reflexes and coordination. Understanding how the eye works helps to improve the coordination of the eye with the rest of the body.

Once you understand that your visual world is framed by your physical limits, you can begin to study what goes on within that framework. It helps to know the basic anatomy of the eyeball. The following diagram is simplified to show the most significant parts.

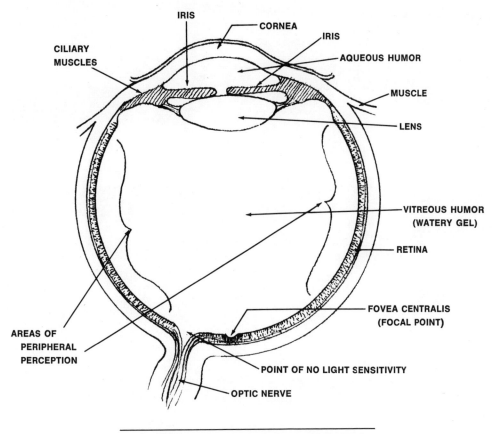

IRIS
CORNEA
IRIS
AQUEOUS HUMOR
CILIARY MUSCLES
MUSCLE
LENS
VITREOUS HUMOR (WATERY GEL)
RETINA
FOVEA CENTRALIS (FOCAL POINT)
AREAS OF PERIPHERAL PERCEPTION
POINT OF NO LIGHT SENSITIVITY
OPTIC NERVE

HORIZONTAL CROSS SECTION OF THE EYEBALL.

Reflected light or direct light enters the eye, passing through the cornea, iris, and lens, where it is filtered and focused so that it is projected onto the retina in an inverted and reversed position. The cone and rod nerve endings of the retina contain a light-sensitive chemical that bleaches out when light strikes it. This reaction causes the nerve endings to send impulses through the optic nerve to the optical centers in the back of the brain. There, through a process that is not fully understood, the impulses are changed into the right-side-up images you see. That's the physical process in a nutshell.

The process of understanding and reading information is accomplished by the brain. You pick up light with your eyes and cycle that information through the mind to test its importance and possible use. Almost all information is either discarded or filed for future use, but once in a while the eye-to-mind system locks in on visual information and it suggests something new and inventive. The basketball player sees a new angle of approach to the basket or the artist sees his world in a new way.

We must no longer ignore the physical aspects of seeing. Conscious understanding of the function of the eyes (visual apperception) offers a greater range of possibilities for the eye-to-mind system. It begins with focusing your attention on your vision and seeing the structure of that image. You see the outside world within the framework of yourself.

The Field of Vision

From the earlier demonstrations, you know that your nose, eyebrows, cheeks, temples, eyelids, and glasses frame everything you see. Within that frame is your field of vision.

The framework is like a picture frame and the field of vision is like the picture inside. You can visually separate the boundaries from the field of vision just as you can remove the strips of wood that border a picture. The earlier demonstrations are intended to help you do that. Now you will be shown ways to see the structure of the field of vision.

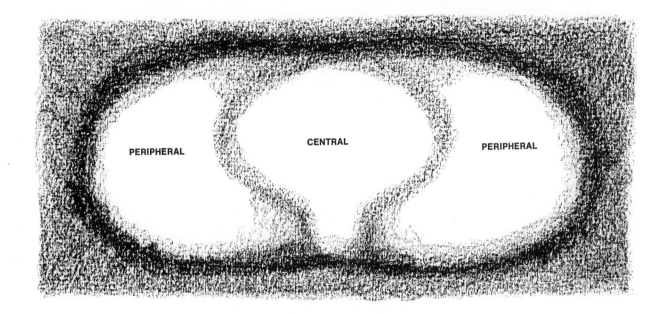

You don't usually see them, but the visual frame divides the field into areas of central and peripheral perception.

Central perception sees the world sharply, clearly, and in depth.

In contrast, peripheral perception is flat and blurred, but it can detect large shapes, strong contrasts, and bold movements.

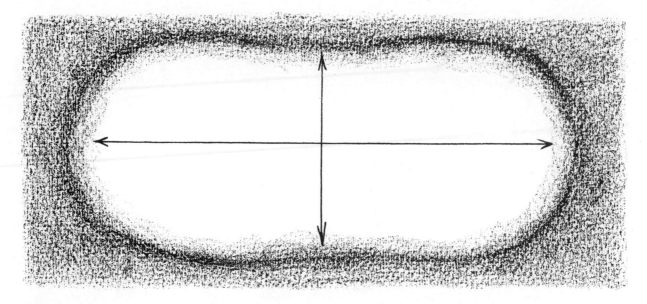

The complete field is horizontal, an oval, more than twice as wide as it is high.

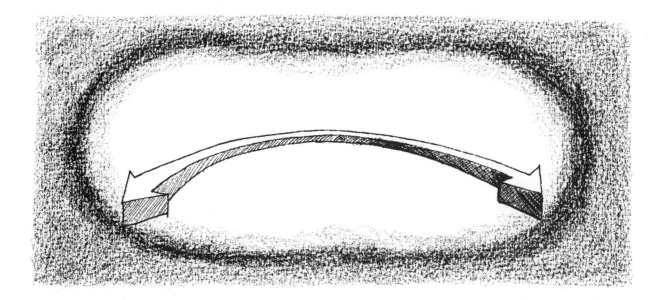

The field curves around to give the peripheral (side) vision that is so important to your perception of movement. You would be a poor and dangerous driver without it.

Try to imagine all the oval field drawings here as large movie screens that curve around your eyes or as wrap-around goggles with drawings on them.

The Focal Point

Take a deep breath.

Shut your eyes.

Breathing smoothly and normally, open your eyes.

Look directly at the spot below.

.

Your ability to see that spot sharply and clearly is the result of the function of the fovea (fovea centralis), a highly sensitive, very small area of light perception within the central region of the retina at the back of the eyeball. It is the key to clear vision.

Unless you have a serious eye defect, you have a fovea. When you see the spot clearly, you are using your fovea to focus your visual system on one point—the focal point.

Walking to school one morning when I was a ten-year-old, I looked up at a telephone wire to see a bird, and for the first time realized I had one small area of vision that made it possible for me to zero in on that bird and see it clearly. For weeks I walked around zapping birds with my focal point. My answer to the beebee gun.

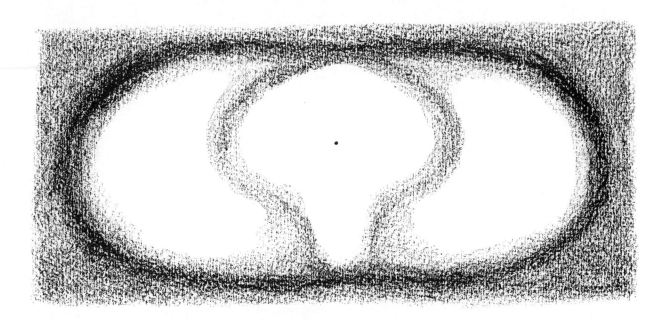

CENTRAL LOCATION OF THE FOCAL POINT WITHIN THE FIELD OF VISION.

The focal point is in the center of your field of vision, but it tends to move constantly, showing you a sharp, clear image of the world.

As you read the words on this page, it is your focal point that follows the words. It can also move in and out of space, focusing as close as six inches from your face to as far out as infinity.

Your visual focus is closely tied to your mind's ability to focus on one idea or thought at a time. As you direct your consciousness to your focal point and away from it, you are also controlling your mental processes and becoming more aware of how to focus your attention. A good way to snap out of a mental fog during a boring situation is to concentrate your focal point on what you are supposed to be looking at. Pick out one small point and try to see it with absolute clarity; the effort will instantly redirect your total attention.

Concentrate your full visual attention on the spot within the circles below.

Try to become more conscious of the small circle and then the large circle without moving your focal point from the spot.

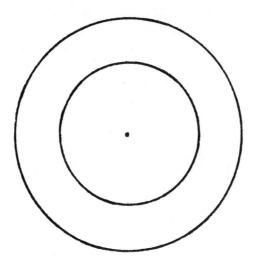

You will find that you have to apply some mental control or your focal point will quite naturally jump out to the circles to see them clearly. It may take some practice. If you try too hard, you may not be able to do it. Be carefree about it. Let your eyes work naturally, and just keep them on the spot as your mind accepts the less clear image of the circles.

The fovea is the only part of the retina that is capable of seeing with maximum clarity. So the circles appear less and less distinct, slightly blurred, the farther they are from the focal point.

Actually, there are two focal points, one functioning within each eye. Try to see the focal point within each eye.

Cover your right eye.

Using only your left eye, concentrate on one spot somewhere out in front of you, and then begin moving your focal point from one spot to another as if you were following the hands of a clock.

Move your focal point in as large a circle as possible, stopping momentarily at spots that interest you.

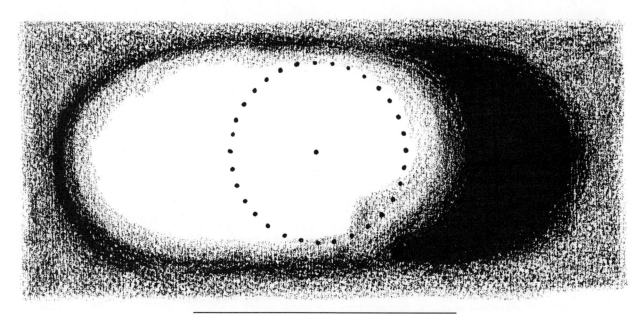

RANGE OF MOVEMENT OF THE LEFT FOCAL POINT.

Now cover your left eye and repeat the same movements with the focal point of the right eye.

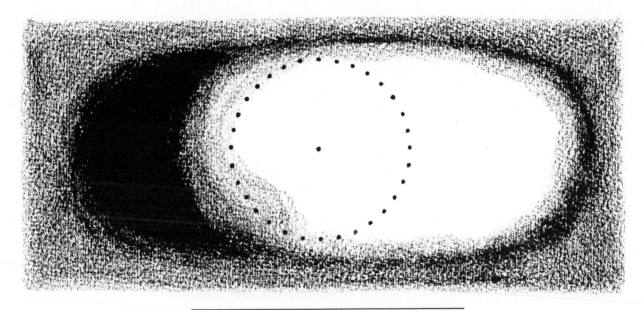

RANGE OF MOVEMENT OF THE RIGHT FOCAL POINT.

Perhaps you noticed that you couldn't move your focal point all the way to the edge of your field of vision. If you place a dot on the drawing of the visual field to represent each stop your focal point made as it followed its largest circle, then you have mapped that area of the visual field in which the focal point functions. It is your depth perception field, and incidentally, it is roughly the same as the central area framed by your two noses.

Open both eyes.

Focus on one part of the circle below and move your focal point around that circle.

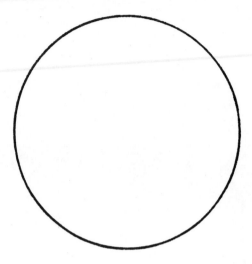

The focal point jumps from one point to another. The muscles that move your eyes move in small jumps when they are directed at still objects.

If you concentrate for a moment on the feeling within the muscles, you will become aware of the minute jumps and starts as you move your focus from one point to another.

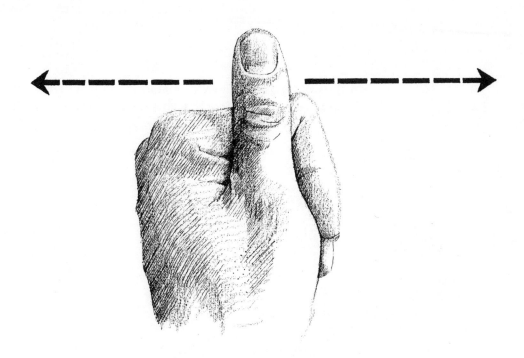

Now hold up your thumb and move it horizontally back and forth.

Follow it with your focal point.

Your eye muscles move smoothly as they follow your thumb. The focal point is capable of smooth movement when you direct it toward a moving object, but it moves rapidly in stops and starts when it scans a still scene.

Your eyes will also move smoothly when not focused, but try as you may, it's almost impossible for your focal point to move smoothly over a still object; yet it moves smoothly when following something in motion.

Covering your left eye and holding up your thumb, focus your right eye directly on an object in the distance beyond your thumb.

Your thumb appears blurry and less clear than the object in the background. Peripheral objects are also blurry and get more blurry the farther they are from your focal point.

Repeat the procedure for the left eye.

Cover your right eye.

Hold out your left thumb.

Focus your left eye directly on your thumb.

All objects in your field of vision beyond your thumb are less clear, just as your thumb was less clear when you focused on the distance.

Repeat the procedure for the right eye.

Night Vision

At night your fovea doesn't function as well as it does in sunlight. It takes as much as forty-five minutes for your eyes to completely adjust to the dark.

Even though your eyes have adjusted, your fovea won't be able to see as clearly as in daylight. If you choose a star or small light in the distance to focus on at night, it will not be as clearly seen with the fovea as it will if you look slightly to one side of it.

The cones scattered throughout the retina work during lighted situations and are found in greater numbers in the fovea; the rods, which work during dim light, hardly exist within the fovea, but are thickly distributed within the areas around the fovea. This explains why a sailor learns to spot lights and stars at night by shifting his focal point slightly away from what he wants to see.

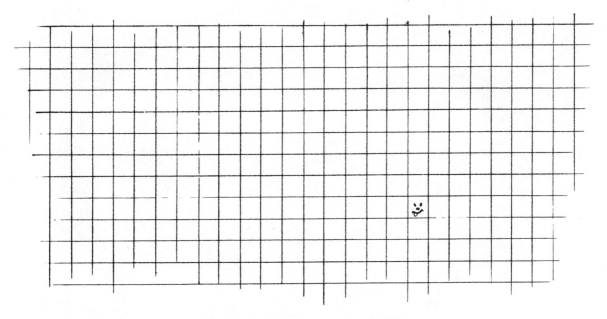

While not perfect, your focal point generally does a good job of pinpointing interesting objects. Without it you probably wouldn't have all those fine little things like jewelry, transistors, and sewing needles. Threading a needle or splitting a diamond would be impossible.

More than any other part of yourself, the focal point functions selectively under the close control of the mind and rejects the dull and boring in favor of the curious, interesting, exciting, and dangerous aspects of your environment.

As you develop an awareness of its abilities, you will enrich your sensitivity to the details of the world. You will develop an increased sense of visual clarity that is a counterpoint to the slightly blurred visual field, and that sense of clarity will be soothing and reassuring.

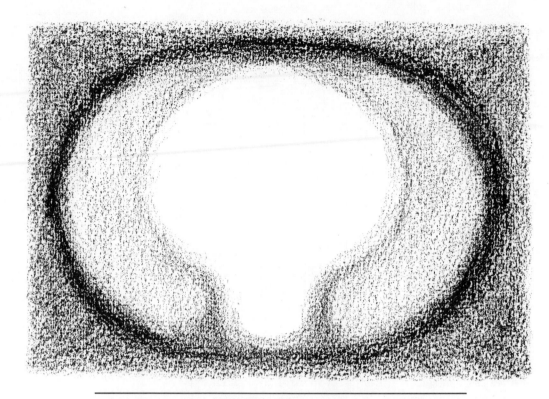

THE PSYCHOLOGICAL IMPORTANCE OF THE CENTRAL AREA OF VISION.

The focal point and the central area of vision in which it moves is so vital to your very survival that, psychologically, you see it as much larger in proportion to the peripheral areas.

It is so essential that a subjective comparison drawing shows the central area to be almost absurdly oversized. Yet, this is the way you see in your mind's eye—the way the brain values the information it receives. That's why you have a hard time seeing the focal point as the very tiny area it really is. Psychologically you resist overthrowing the accumulated power of experience of the visual center of your brain and refuse to let your eyes go back to a primal state of simple perception.

A Camera Doesn't Have a Focal Point

THE CAMERA CLEARLY RECORDS THE OBJECTS THAT FALL WITHIN THE FOCAL PLANE. OTHERS IN THE FOREGROUND AND BACKGROUND ARE OUT OF FOCUS.

TO SIMULATE A FOCAL POINT, THE CAMERA IS ADJUSTED TO INCLUDE ONLY ONE AREA OF INTEREST WITHIN THE FOCAL PLANE.

THE FOCAL PLANE (DEPTH OF FIELD) IS OUTLINED AS IT IS SEEN BY THE CAMERA THAT SHOT THESE PICTURES. IN SNAPSHOT CAMERAS THE DEPTH OF FIELD IS FIXED, BUT IT CAN BE INCREASED OR DECREASED IN CAMERAS WITH ADJUSTABLE LENSES.

A quick comparison of the eye and the camera will help you appreciate the unique and special quality of your eyes.

The eye has a focal point created by the fovea, and the camera has a focal plane created by its lens and the flat film surface. The camera cannot really pick out one point of interest and focus intensely on it. It picks out a plane like a pane of glass in a window in front of the camera. The plane is parallel to the film in the back of the camera. Anything that falls on or within the thickness of that plane is equally reproduced in focus. The thickness of that plane is called the depth of focal field (depth of field, for short), and it can be controlled by the aperture opening on cameras with adjustable lenses. Of course, the photographer can create the illusion of a focal point simply by arranging his camera so that no other object falls within the focal plane, but even then the single tiny point of intense clarity is just not there.

Stereoscopic Vision

Depth perception comes mainly from stereoscopic vision. In order to see this function follow the next three demonstrations.

Hold up your thumb and look directly at an imaginary spot on your thumbnail.

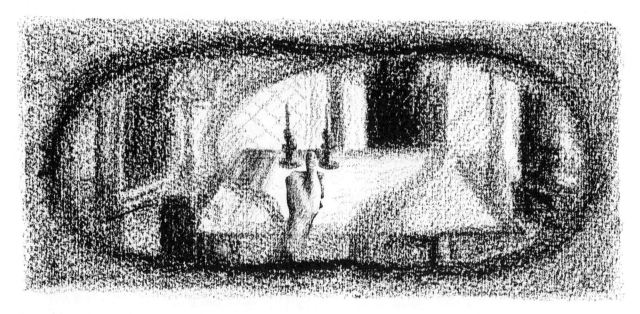

You should be able to see two blurry versions of the object beyond your thumb in the background.

Keep your thumb extended and fix your focal point on a distant object.

You should be able to see two blurry thumbs off to the sides of the focal point.

Shifting the focal point quickly back and forth from the distant object to the thumb gives you a means of judging the distance between the two. The farther apart your two thumbs appear (or your two noses, for that matter) the farther in the distance your focus is.

Of course, it is stereoscopic vision that produces the two-nose effect. The distance between the two gives you a built-in aid to depth perception. The closer to your eyes that you focus, the closer together the two noses come.

Your two eyes give you two slightly different vantage points. The two different views overlap within your mind's eye and come together exactly only at the focal point. The slight differences between what one eye sees and what the other eye sees give you a feeling for the distances between objects up to twenty feet away from your eyes.

If you choose an object somewhere out in front of you, and you hold up one thumb at arm's length and the other about twelve inches from your nose, you can see the disparity in the two views by looking at the farther thumb.

The closest thumb becomes two and the object in the distance beyond the other thumb becomes two; both are slightly out of focus and appear to be transparent. The doubling is the chief effect of stereoscopic vision.

A peculiar quality of stereoscopic vision is that the two separate images seen by the eyes don't really blend into one equal image. There is a rivalry between the eyes for dominance, and one eye is usually dominant most of the time just as the right or the left hand is dominant. Most people who wear glasses know that one eye is stronger than the other because their lenses are ground to correct the error within each individual eye. This closely relates to the tendency for one eye to dominate the other. The dominant eye usually sees more accurately.

If you present an object to one eye exclusively and another object to the other eye, you see an attempted mixture of the two objects by the brain. The image of the dominant eye appears to float in front of the other image or obscure it altogether. The two objects may mix for you if you concentrate on seeing them both equally clearly, but you won't get a perfect mixture. With practice, you can shift your attention from one eye to the other. Think "left eye" and its image will dominate. Think "right eye" and its image will dominate. It's difficult but not impossible.

Hold the bottom edge of this page about one inch away from the bottom of your nose so that your nostrils cover the triangle.

Let your eyes focus out past the page so that the horizontal and vertical lines cross each other (they will be blurry).

Concentrate on your left eye to make the horizontals dominant, and concentrate on your right eye to make the verticals dominant.

It is possible to incorporate the stereoscopic function of your eyes into photography by making use of the rivalry between the left and right eye. The technique itself was invented about 1838 by the English physicist Charles Wheatstone and was later used by David Brewster to create the stereoscope (stereopticon) commonly found as a novelty item in turn-of-the-century parlors. It has evolved into the present-day 3-D movies and was used by Apollo astronauts to bring back photographs that would capture some of the feeling for the distance between objects on the lunar landscape.

The technique requires that two photographs be taken simultaneously. This is done with a camera that has two lenses that are approximately the same distance apart as the pupils of a person's eyes. The two lenses expose two different pictures side-by-side on the film (opposite page). The resulting photograph on the left is shown only to the left eye and the photograph on the right is shown only to the right eye. This can be accomplished by several different complicated mechanical means involving colored or polarized filters (as in 3-D movies), or by physically separating the two photographs with a viewer held close to the eyes. Each picture copies a slightly different view of its subject. You can see this in the third photograph which is a facsimile of how the two would look if they could be successfully overlapped. The reason this print doesn't appear to be three-dimensional is because it lacks the retinal rivalry of the optical center of the brain. We can't reproduce that technique here, but the print does indicate the disparity between the two different angles of view. The preceding three exercises are intended to help you see that disparity between the images of your two eyes.

Stereophotography still has a focal plane rather than a focal point and lacks the panoramic scope of human peripheral vision. We've learned some ingenious methods of simulating some of the functions of the eyes, but it's all the more incredible that our eyes have the ability to adapt psychologically and make sense of pictures that are only vaguely reminiscent of the natural eye-to-mind process.

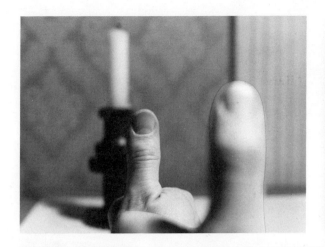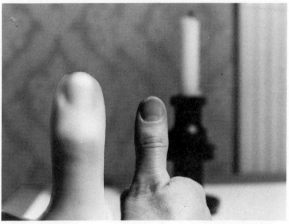

IN THESE SIMULATED STEREO PHOTOGRAPHS, WHICH HAVE BEEN SLIGHTLY EXAGGERATED FOR EASIER COMPREHENSION, THE PHOTO ON THE LEFT REPRESENTS WHAT THE LEFT LENS OF A STEREO CAMERA WOULD SEE AND THE RIGHT-HAND PHOTO WHAT THE RIGHT LENS WOULD SEE.

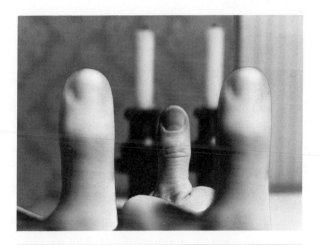

THIS IS HOW THE DISPARITY BETWEEN THE TWO PHOTOGRAPHS APPEARS IF THEY COULD BE OVER-LAPPED. THE CAMERA FOCUSES ITS TWO LENSES ON THE THUMB IN THE MIDDLE DISTANCE, SO THE THUMB CLOSEST TO THE LENSES AND THE CANDLE IN THE BACKGROUND ARE DOUBLE.

Floaters

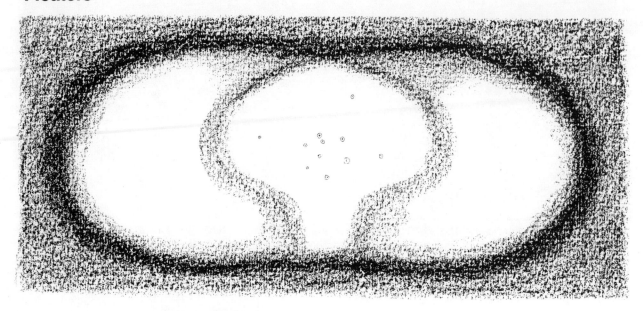

Gaze at the sky.

Let your eyes relax. Look at nothing in particular.

Adopt a daydreaming state of mind.

Spots will appear to float in front of your eyes, but if you try to look at them directly they will move out of the way.

The floating spots cannot be seen by the focal point, because, as a part of the eye, they move when the focal point moves. They appear to dash out of the way each time you try to see them clearly.

The spots are minute alterations in the vitreous fluid that fills the area between the cornea and the iris. Appropriately, they are called floaters.

Afterimages

The rods and cones within the retina contain photopigments that react to light by bleaching out and sending nerve impulses to the brain. If too much light hits those elements, they bleach out more thoroughly and take longer to return to normal. The image of the light, like a flashbulb that pops in your face, lingers on as an afterimage, and it reappears when you close your eyes.

A color afterimage, which is more subtle, can be produced by staring for a minute or more at a simple color patch laid against a plain ground of a different color. The afterimage is the visual complement to the color seen, and it can be seen by quickly shifting your focus over to a solid white ground.*

The following instructions will help you see different kinds of ordinary afterimages.

Light a candle in a dark room and sit about four feet away, keeping the flame at eye level.

Close your eyes, cover them with the cupped palms of your hands, and relax for a few seconds. Remove your hands, but keep your eyes closed.

Look at the candle flame and quickly open and close your eyes, leaving them open for no more than a second at a time.

When you close your eyes (cover them with your palms for best effect) you still see an image of the candle flame, which fades away in about ten seconds.

---

* For more on color afterimages, see Josef Albers. *Interaction of Color*. New Haven, Yale Univ. Press, 1971.

Repeat the same procedures, but open your eyes, look at the flame, and then move your eyes around for about two seconds—any movement works. Close your eyes and cover them with your palms.

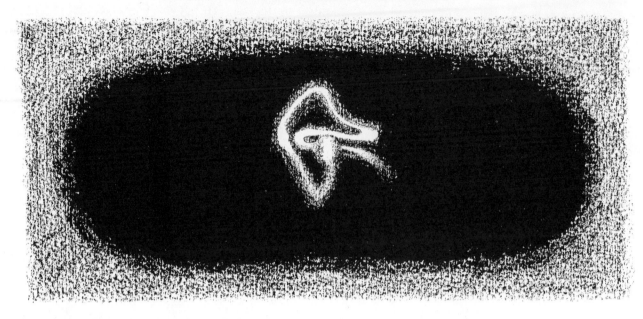

The lighted squiggles and streaks are the captured motion of the light in the form of an afterimage.

Again, repeat the same procedures, but when you look at the candle, hold your focal point directly on the flame for approximately one minute. Blink when necessary, but keep staring at the flame. Close your eyes and cover them with your palms.

A light afterimage of the flame appears and lingers much longer than in the earlier exercises. If you are very quiet and attentive while your eyes are closed, you can watch the afterimage gradually change colors—sometimes violet, but slowly becoming deeper red—until it becomes a dark image and slowly disappears.

And again, repeat the same procedure as before, staring at the flame for one minute or more. Blink when necessary.

Look directly at a large white surface that is well lighted. Stare at it for one minute.

Appearing light at first, the afterimage quickly turns dark, but if you look at a dark surface, the spot appears light. The light, or positive, afterimage occurs because the bleached rods and cones in the retina continue to send responses through the optic nerve to the brain. The dark, or negative, afterimage occurs as those same rods and cones become less responsive until they are restored. The brighter the light, the stronger the afterimage. If the light is too bright, the afterimage can become permanant.

Staring at the sun can cause blindness. Besides overbleaching, the rods and cones can get burned and may never again function properly. Snow blindness occurs because most of the retina has become damaged by glaring light reflecting off the snow. Wise skiers protect themselves by blackening their cheeks and wearing sunglasses. Welders, too, must shield their eyes from the hot and glaring torch as much as from the flying sparks.

All of us must guard against careless curiosity when a solar eclipse occurs. Staring directly into the darkened sun, even through sunglasses or exposed film, can be dangerous. The sun may be blocked, but its harmful ultraviolet rays aren't, and they can blind you. Worse, there is none of the usual pain your eyes would feel from staring into regular sunlight. So you won't have that warning signal that tells you your eyes are in danger. If you ever feel pain from looking into a light, and you're having difficulty keeping your eyes open, turn your eyes away. Never stare into the sun.

There is a way to view a solar eclipse safely. Punch a tiny hole in a piece of paper. Hold another piece of paper under the first piece and move the top paper back and forth until you get the sun focused through the hole, so that its image appears on the paper underneath. That way you can see the moon's shadow block out the sun without ruining your eyes.

Ordinarily, unless you have some special problems, you don't need sunglasses in average sunlight. Nor do you need them indoors, no matter what the going fashion. Their frames obscure your peripheral vision, and the dark lenses alter color perception. However, they are excellent for fighting glare and should be used for that purpose, particularly if you have to drive a car in bright sunlight.

Hopefully, you now have a basic knowledge of your own visual sense. It's not my intention to present visual material that makes you feel like a fool for not being able to see what you are supposed to see. For that reason, I have omitted optical illusions and other unexplainable tricks of vision, which are fascinating but distracting.

The preceding demonstrations deal mostly with physical rather than psychological aspects of vision, in order to make a total seeing experience as simple as possible. However, that does not mean you have experienced all the demonstrations as planned. It may take time and more effort. Rather than worry about the things you couldn't see, feel good that you accomplished some of the exercises and discovered something more about yourself.

Even though the visual process is mostly reflexive and automatic, it is possible for you consciously to control your visual responses. Open your eyes and see. Total awareness, openness, and a calm relaxed mind are essential to deeper seeing experiences, and will in turn reinforce those qualities. Your eyes will give you personal experiences you never imagined.

3 / Exercising Your Sense of Seeing

I was meandering through a used-book store, trying to find something to read, when I happened to notice a book by Aldous Huxley entitled *The Art of Seeing.* I had admired since college his *Doors of Perception* and *Heaven and Hell,* so looking over *The Art of Seeing* convinced me it was exactly the kind of book that would help me better understand the nature of vision.

Among many other things, Huxley was concerned with the development of the full potential of the mind, particularly the mind's control over the functions of the body. *The Art of Seeing* was written in defense of Dr. William H. Bates's method of improving eyesight without the use of glasses. Dr. Bates was an ophthalmologist who pioneered exercise techniques to improve vision and wrote *Better Eyesight Without Glasses* in the 1920's. After a rare illness had almost completely blinded Huxley in his late teens, he began the Bates program of eye exercises and eventually regained his vision. This may have contributed to his lifelong concern with mental processes, a concern that included the unconscious influence of the mind over the body as well as the mind's ability to alter its own perceptions. Huxley believed that the body often becomes ill or loses its ability to function properly because the mind is not properly tuned, fear and anxiety being the chief culprits. In *The Art of Seeing,* he expresses the belief that the eyes are equally affected by mental malfunctions.

Several months later, I located a copy of Bates's book and found it to be true to Huxley's description. The point was made that the exercises would help keep a person's eyes in shape and help prevent defects that come from aging and misuse. Even though my vision is good (20/20), I began doing many of the exercises and include some of them in the following material. I have met people who no longer wear glasses as a result of Bates's exercises, and I have met others who wear glasses but continue exercise at the suggestion of their doctors. Eye exercises are more commonly known and practiced than you might believe.

After my study of Huxley and Bates, I became interested in yoga and found that there are very similar hatha yoga eye exercises that have been used for thousands of years. Both approaches point out the need for releasing tension to achieve the best results during the exercises. The body must be relaxed, and the mind must be geared down or as blank as possible, yet open and awake.

Recently, I was fortunate enough to talk with some people* who have traveled in the People's Republic of China in the last few years. They told me about their tours of schools and factories, where they saw people practicing eye exercises in addition to daily total exercise routines. At an embroidery factory where workers were sewing in fine detail with human hair, an American asked why so few of the workers wore glasses. The worker-guide told of the active involvement the people have with their own health care and explained that they were able to prevent the need for glasses, in most cases, by taking regular breaks for eye exercises (discussed later). This incident was typical of the stories Americans related about their visits to many Chinese schools. Apparently, the whole culture takes the idea of preventing eye disorders very seriously. Their involvement with good eye care is in marked contrast to the behavior of people in Western cultures, who resist efforts at maintaining good vision. We need to study the Chinese techniques and adopt a program of regular eye exercises as well as other health-maintainance routines for the rest of the body. We have nothing to lose, and we won't know what we have to gain until we try.

My chief concerns are actually with those creative people who are pushing for the achievement of total human potential both socially and individually. I believe we are at a stage where we can begin to establish controls over the quality of our own evolution. Many of us are seeking ways to prevent the unnatural deterioration of our minds and bodies, and we hope for the day the medical profession adopts the concept of prevention of disease as its primary goal.

In any effort for self-improvement, our senses should be given extra attention because it is through them that we learn about ourselves and our functions. We have to keep a regular check on our senses because they may be warning us of problems beyond themselves, just as astronauts have to keep track of warning lights on their instrument panels. Since our vision is our most used sense, it seems logical that we should start by checking out our eyes with eye examinations, then learn to care for them properly and give them the best possible exercise.

* Thanks to Rachel Burger, who originally suggested I look into the Chinese eye exercises, and to John Dove of Science for People, Frances Crow of American Friends Service Committee, Carol Rosen of U.S.–China Peoples' Friendship Association. Special thanks to Kathy Lazarus and Julie Hu of U.S.–China Peoples' Friendship Association for their translation of these exercises.

About the Exercises

The purpose of eye exercises is to stretch and contract the muscles that surround the eyeball and the tiny muscles that control the internal lens of the eye. A regular routine of exercise helps make 20/20 eyes more alert by increasing the awareness of the peripheral area of vision and the clarity of the focal point; reflex responses can be sharpened and eye fatigue can be controlled by learning to bring the eyes to a completely relaxed state of rest during times of strain. The exercises can improve the appearance of the eyes by controlling eyeball redness, dark rings, and bags that are the results of strain and exhaustion.

Exercises can also help improve some cases of poor vision, if they are followed religiously each day with the proper attitude of concentration and relaxation. However, improvement of common defects is usually tedious and slow. The best results are achieved if the exercises are followed under the close direction of an ophthalmologist who is sympathetic to the use of eye exercises and who has a good understanding of the exact nature of the defect. Without the help of an exercise-oriented eye doctor, you can expect only minimal physical improvement. Many ophthalmologists and optometrists believe the only way to improve vision is to prescribe glasses, so if you are interested in exercises, look carefully for the right doctor and ask questions.

Only one type of ocular deficiency is universally thought by the profession to respond to exercises—strabismus (crossed eyes and walleyes). The muscles of one eye weaken, keeping it from working in conjunction with the other eye. The exercises are called orthoptic training and are sometimes prescribed along with glasses.

In spite of the many people who have improved their vision with exercises, the controversy still rages concerning the use of exercises for other relatively minor eye defects, such as nearsightedness, farsightedness, and defects due to aging. The National Society for the Prevention of Blindness still maintains that eye exercises are probably of no help, except in the one case previously mentioned. Yet, if you consult doctors who are not prejudiced by their belief that glasses are the only means of correcting visual problems, you find that many of them readily prescribe exercises, and some prescribe glasses along with an exercise program or even suggest that you wear your glasses only when you need them. In some cases, glasses and exercises are designed to work together so that eventually the glasses can be discarded. However, in the vast majority of cases, glasses are prescribed with every intention that they will be permanent nose ornaments.

New findings in the field may be useful in developing future visual therapy techniques. Lyall Watson mentions in his book *Super Nature* that hypnosis has been used experimentally to improve nearsightedness (myopia). Hypnosis enables an individual to respond to suggestions that control his autonomic (involuntary) functions—in this case, by changing the shape of the eyeball. Recently, I talked with psychologist Buryl Payne, author of *Getting There Without Drugs,* who is working with alpha-wave biofeedback equipment to help induce a state of hypnosis or deep relaxation. He told me he has been able to improve his own myopia and gradually decrease the strength of his glasses by using the Bates program combined with self-hypnosis. It would be good if these and other individual efforts could be applied on a wider scale to develop even better methods for improving poor vision.

In this context, let me tell you more of what I've been able to find out about the Chinese exercises. These exercises are oriented primarily toward relaxing the muscles around the eyes by the use of finger massage at pressure points that are similar to acupuncture needle points. This is done for fifteen minutes twice a day and always with the eyes closed. During the exercises, one sits quietly and listens to music.

The Chinese are taught to sit up straight while reading, not to read while lying down, and to read or do close work only in well-lighted situations. In elementary school classrooms, posters remind the children that eye care is important to good health. Eye examinations are made regularly by doctors or trained paraprofessionals. At the middle school level, children are taught the anatomy of the eye, and they learn that knowledge of the eye's function, along with regular attention to preventive care, is vital to good health.

Recent correspondence* with the People's Republic of China indicates that studies of the eye exercise programs have shown good results. For example, the Bienmen Primary School in Fongcheng county, Liaoning Province, has two hundred pupils at the second-year level, thirty-seven (18.4% of the total) had weakening vision. After a regular program of eye exercises, twenty-five pupils (67% of the original thirty-seven) had their eyesight returned to normal.

My hope is that this information will spark some real interest in this country in preventing visual problems. I would like to see a serious long-range program like China's adopted in our schools to help us learn how to keep our eyes in good health.

We depend so heavily on our eyes that most of us fear we may easily damage them. We think of them as if they were little TV or movie cameras, mechanical devices, when they are in fact made of living tissues that are as much a part of our bodies as our fingers and toes. If exercises can help maintain the health of the body, then why not the health of the eyes. I recommend Huxley's *Art of Seeing* and Bates's *Better Eyesight Without Glasses* if you have doubts or want to try more exercises on your own to

---

* Thanks to the Chinese People's Association for Friendship with Foreign Countries for a prompt response to my request for these statistics. This may be the first Western publication of statistical information to back up the theory of using eye exercises to prevent visual problems in the classroom.

correct poor vision. A more contemporary book is now available which discusses exercises and gives pointers on preventing eye problems. It is *How To Improve Your Vision* by Robert A. Kraskin. Kraskin's book updates the Bates method and puts some of Bates's exaggerated claims into proper perspective. Some of Bates's exercises, like reading in poor light and glancing into the sun, have been discredited, but many of his ideas are still valuable.*

In no way do I mean to suggest that diseases such as glaucoma or cataracts can be cured with eye exercises. They cannot. Anyone who attempts these or other exercises to correct serious eye diseases can do great harm to their eyes by delaying proper medical care. There is no way for you to tell a serious disease from a minor defect without a professional examination. So have checkups regularly.

Eye exercises can, however, help to develop an inner awareness of the world of visual experience, and thus can improve vision physically and aesthetically, by expanding the consciousness of subliminal visual perceptions.

Approaching the Exercises

Some people seem to lack the ability to respond to any form of physical exercise or the patience to stick with it. A few have become quite disturbed by the exercises in this book. When I asked them to tell me what the trouble was, they stated that the exercises made them more self-conscious of their eyes and their bodies. The experience was negative because it directly confronted their doubts about their bodily performance. Those doubts were based on competitive feelings of accomplishment and they defeated the efforts of the would-be exercisers.

Most people have little trouble responding positively if they approach the exercises slowly and properly perform the rest and concentration breaks which appear throughout the book (the black ovals). If you find it difficult, I suggest that you try a little each day so that you move through the book at a leisurely pace. Attempting all the exercises at the first sitting can be frustrating. If it helps, the order of the exercises can be rearranged as you feel the need. The approach should be made in a calm meditative state of mind—a state of self-hypnosis is best. Set aside a particular time each day in a quiet place so you can make the most of each exercise.

Think of the exercises as aesthetic experiences, like listening to music or visiting a museum. Imagine that you are painting or drawing with your eyes as you follow the exercises. An eye movement might be a brush stroke added to other strokes that "paint" a picture in your mind's eye.

---

* For information on exercise-oriented optometrists, Kraskin suggests you write to: Chairman, Committee on Orthoptics and Visual Training, American Optometric Association, 7000 Chippewa Street, St. Louis, Missouri, 63119.

Don't expect physical results too soon. If you are overconcerned with physical improvements, you will go around looking at things you have had trouble seeing expecting to see them better. Those very expectations create enough tension and anxiety to keep your eyes from seeing clearly. Instead, concentrate on all the new things you never noticed before. Feel the excitement of discovering within yourself the inner being that perceives, feels, and thinks. Let yourself enjoy the total seeing experience.

Concentrate.

Choose an object and quietly stare at it.

Blinking whenever necessary, try to absorb the whole scene, the total field of vision, without moving your focal point away from that object.

This involves mind control as well as eye control, a state of absorbing consciousness. As you concentrate your focus, you must try to expand your attention so that it allows you to become conscious of peripheral vision without moving your focal point. The next two exercises should help you develop this ability.

Move your hands together slowly from positions over your shoulders. Look directly at them only after they have come together at your focal point.

Since your peripheral vision areas detect movement best, your moving hands will help you become conscious of those areas. Practice helps.

Explore. Look straight ahead without moving your focal point. Hold your hands up at eye level over your shoulders and move them back and forth until you can see them disappear and reappear within your peripheral fields.

When you thoroughly accept the fact that at only one point in your field of vision can you see absolutely clearly, you'll have little trouble absorbing the total scope of your visual field.

This exercise has the advantage of being adaptable to almost any place or circumstance. When you have made enough progress to drop the hand movements, you can do the exercise on the bus or train, or at work, or school. You don't have to worry about attracting a crowd because no one will have any idea what you are doing. After all, it's a mind-control exercise and there is no reason you can't do it anywhere as long as you can relax and concentrate.

You'll find that stopping your usual collage of thoughts while trying this exercise can clear your head and help control your thinking and your seeing.

Rest.

Rub your hands together until they are warm.

Cup your hands over both eyes without touching the eyes for thirty seconds.

Contemplate.

Let blackness fill your total field of vision.

Your eyelids are too thin to close out all light, and the eyes rest better in a state of total darkness, so use the palms of your hands to block out the light. This is known in yoga and in the Bates method as palming.

Palming also helps to relax the mind and relieve tension. You may find it helpful at odd times even when you are not doing eye exercises.

If you are in a situation where you cannot palm your eyes, just close your eyelids for an extended period and try to imagine total darkness.

Adopt a blank gaze, trying not to focus on any one point, and swing your head from side to side. You will see horizontal streaks of light curving across your field of vision. Faster swinging will produce stronger streaks than slower speeds.

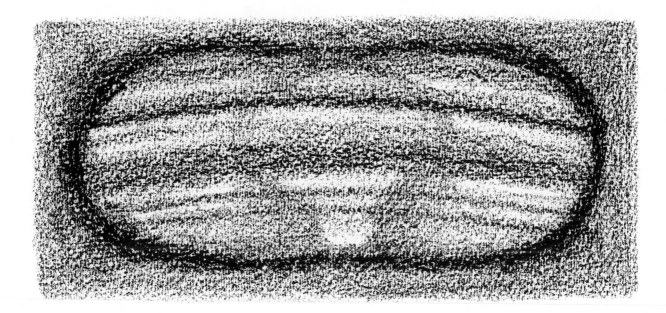

The idea is to take the work load off your focal point. To produce the effect, try not to look directly at the objects that go by.

When you look down at the ground from a moving train or car, you are going so fast that it is impossible to focus on one point passing by. So what you see are continuous streaks zipping by. At slower speeds you can sometimes focus on a pebble and watch it as you move by, or if you try not to focus on the pebble, it will become a streak moving by. At even slower speeds your eyes stop seeing streaks and focus on one pebble after another, following one for a while and then jumping to another.

Moving your head at different speeds can create all these motion effects.

You can learn to see the streaks with slower and slower turns of your head, just by controlling conscious awareness of your focal point. When you can give up the need to see those objects clearly, you will see the streaks. It's like breaking the bonds of the material world; some people have trouble seeing the streaks because they don't want to let go.

In the same manner, swing your head up and down to produce vertical streaks of light.

These two exercises require that you control the natural tendency to jump your focal point from one object to another as you turn your head. Practically all your seeing involves the direct use of the focal point, and the swinging exercises take the mental attention away from that point and shift it to the total field as it moves by. When you see the streaks, you have achieved a simple form of mental control and will feel confidence in the control of your vision.

Rest.

Palm your eyes.

Hatha Yoga Eye Exercises (*Nethra Vyāyāmam*)

The next four movement diagrams represent my interpretation of hatha yoga eye exercises. They require that you repeatedly look to the boundaries of your field of vision so that the muscles that control the eyeballs are thoroughly stretched and contracted. In fact, you can feel the muscles pulling all the way back to your ears. Since you don't normally exercise your eyes to that extent, be careful not to overdo it. Go slowly. Concentrate on moving your eyes smoothly in the lines and curves described in the diagrams. As you repeat the directions over a period of time, yoga masters claim you will improve your vision as well as your ability to concentrate.

While previous exercises are designed to make your eyes work better, these are also recommended to help them look good. They'll help to eliminate minor redness of the eyes and get rid of the ugly bags under the eyes.

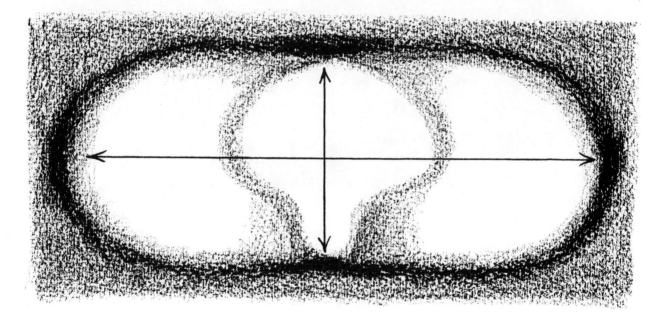

In a state of concentration and relaxation, look straight up and down five times, slowly.

Look from side to side five times. Go slowly.

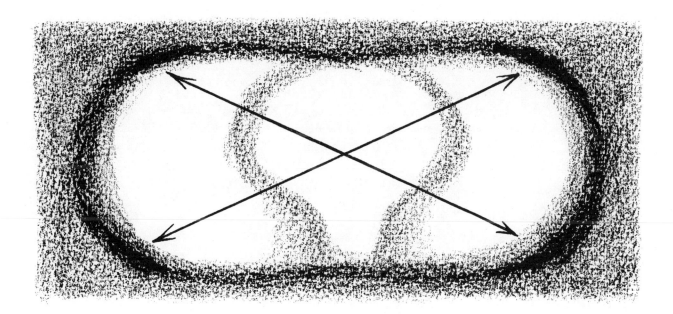

Look diagonally five times each way, slowly.

Concentrate on the stretching of muscles without straining to the point of pain.

Rest.

Palm your eyes.

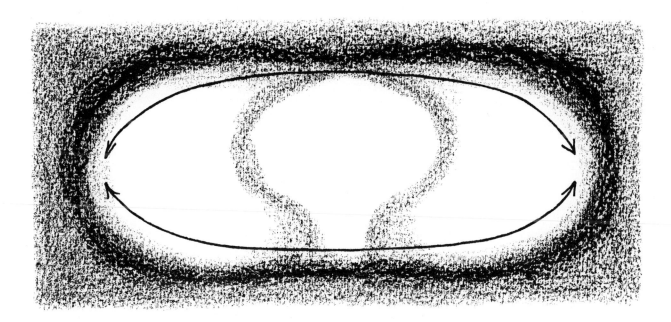

Look up to the top of the frame of your field of vision and move your eyes back and forth in an arch three times, slowly.

Look down at the bottom of your field of vision and rock your eyes back and forth three times, slowly.

Don't try to see any more than the blurry impression of your nose, cheeks, eyebrows, and eyelids.

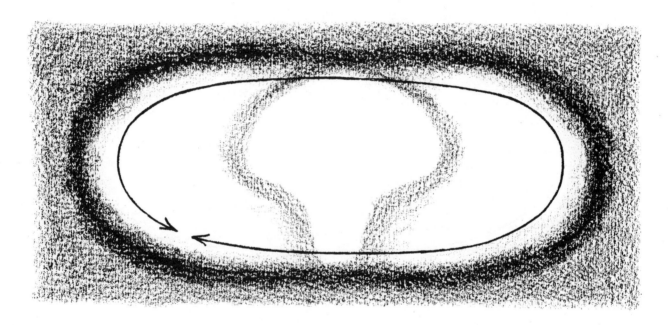

Now, slowly roll your eyes round and round, following the complete frame of your field of vision, three times each way.

When you have fully mastered these movements smoothly, try them with your eyes closed.

78

Rest.

Palm your eyes.

Focal Point Exercise

Hold your thumb out in front of you as far as possible. Focus on a spot on your thumb with both eyes.

While still focusing on your thumb, slowly bring it close to your eyes. When you begin to feel a strain in your eyes, slowly move your thumb back into the distance as you follow it with your eyes.

Repeat five times, slowly.

Rest.

Palm your eyes.

Daily repetition of this exercise helps each eye function better as part of a team of two. It has been suggested for strabismus, a condition in which the eyes lack coordination and tend to wander. It can improve your ability to focus close up because it exercises the tiny internal muscles that control the lens as well as the external muscles that move the eyeball.

You can relieve the eyestrain of continuous reading and increase the time you can spend reading with a simpler variation of this exercise which requires that you look occasionally across the room, focus, palm your eyes for a second, and then return to reading.

Blinking

The eyelids wash the eyes, protect them from too much light, and help prevent injuries from foreign matter. Controlled blinking can help soothe and relax the eyes and the mind and can strengthen eyelid muscles.

Blink your eyes open and shut as rapidly as possible for about ten seconds.

Shut your eyes for ten seconds and then repeat the blinking.

Repeat the cycle three times.

If you blink rapidly enough you will see a fascinating strobelike effect that makes movement flicker like an old movie.

Rest.

Palm your eyes.

When your eyes are closed, reconstruct in your mind's eye the visual impressions that the exercises have given you.

Chinese Eye Exercises

The following Chinese illustrations and translated instructions are tacked up in classrooms to remind the students to practice eye exercises. These are natural routines, reminiscent of the automatic rubbing we do whenever our eyes feel tired. They have grown out of traditional Chinese health care and are based on pressure points, which are pressed and massaged with the fingertips while the eyes are closed.

I suggest that you play music with a simple moderate beat while doing the exercises. Allow about fifteen minutes in the middle of the morning and fifteen minutes in the middle of the afternoon. You will find them especially helpful when your eyes are strained by close work or reading—they are extremely relaxing.

眼保健操图解

注　意　事　项

1.操练时要闭着眼睛做，跟着唱片的速度进行。2.经常剪短指甲，并保持两手的清洁。3.按揉时穴位要准确，手法要轻缓，以各穴位产生酸的感觉为止，不要过分用力，防止压迫眼球。4.一般每天可做两次，上、下午各一次，要坚持经常操练。5.做眼保健操的同时还要注意用眼卫生。

EYE EXERCISE CHART.

Points to attend to:

1. When you exercise, close your eyes, sit quietly, and concentrate. Go according to the speed of the music on the record (recorded music is played during the exercises).

2. Keep your hands clean and your fingernails trimmed.

3. When you press the pressure point you must be accurate, be gentle; press at each point until you feel a kind of ache (what the Chinese call a "sour" feeling). Don't use too much force and avoid putting pressure on the eyeballs.

4. Each day you can exercise twice—once in the morning and once in the afternoon. Be diligent in staying with the routine.

5. Besides doing the exercises, always take care how you use your eyes.

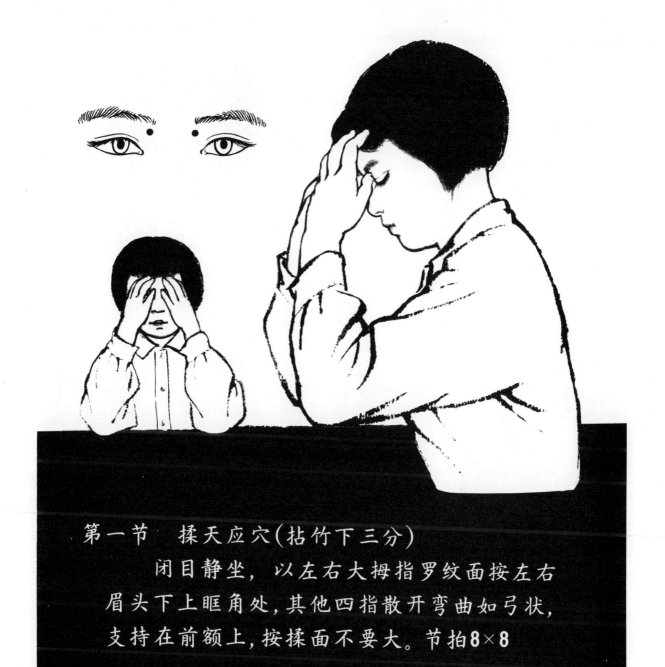

第一节　揉天应穴(拈竹下三分)

　　闭目静坐，以左右大拇指罗纹面按左右
眉头下上眶角处，其他四指散开弯曲如弓状，
支持在前额上，按揉面不要大。节拍8×8

FIRST PART (RELATES TO THE RECORD): STIMULATING THE TIAN YING POINT. THIS POINT IS ABOUT THREE MILLIMETERS BELOW THE ZHAN ZHU POINT (SEE FOURTH PART, POINT 2).

Close your eyes, sit, and concentrate. Put your thumbs below your eyebrows and above the corners of your eyes; spread the other four fingers of each hand and curve your fingers like a bow to support your forehead. The surface you stimulate shouldn't be too large. Press and rub the point to 8 beats of the music (or eight counts). Repeat this eight times.

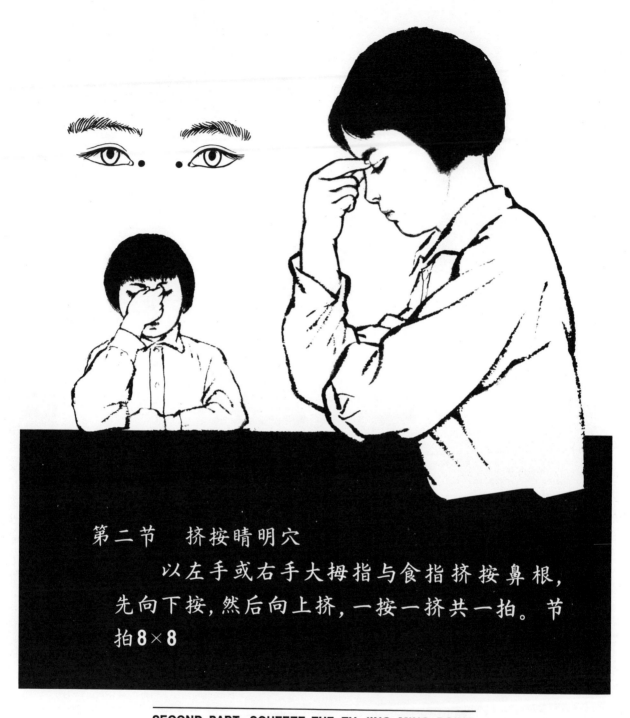

第二节　挤按睛明穴

　　以左手或右手大拇指与食指挤按鼻根，先向下按，然后向上挤，一按一挤共一拍。节拍8×8

SECOND PART: SQUEEZE THE FU JING MING POINT.

Use the thumb and the index finger of either hand to massage the bridge of your nose. First press (the point) and then squeeze with an upward motion. Each press and squeeze equals one count, eight counts equals one cycle. Complete eight cycles (sixty-four presses and squeezes altogether).

84

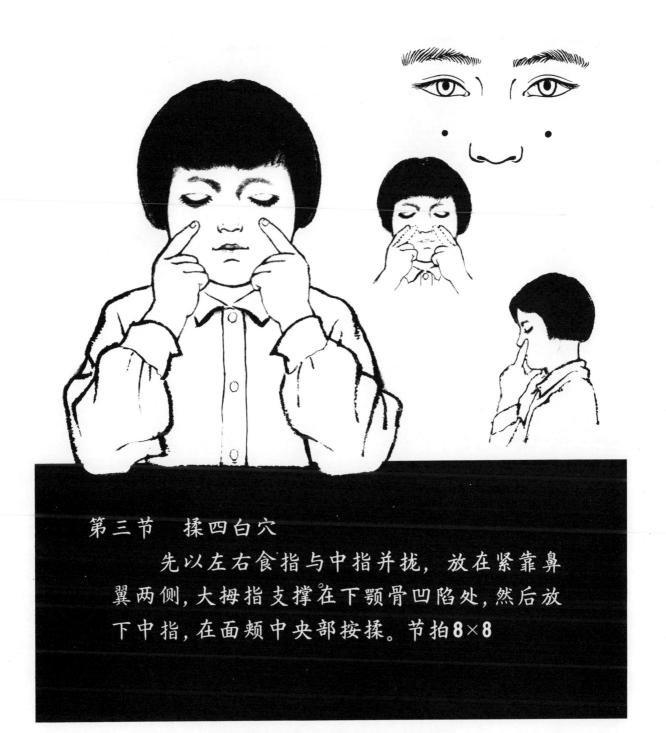

第三节　揉四白穴

　　先以左右食指与中指并拢，放在紧靠鼻翼两侧，大拇指支撑在下颚骨凹陷处，然后放下中指，在面颊中央部按揉。节拍8×8

THIRD PART: RUBBING THE SI BAI POINT.

First put the index and the middle fingers together, place them against either side of the nostrils, supporting your chin on your thumbs. Take down your middle finger (after you have found the Si Bai point with your index finger). Massage the center part of your cheeks for a count of eight and repeat for eight cycles.

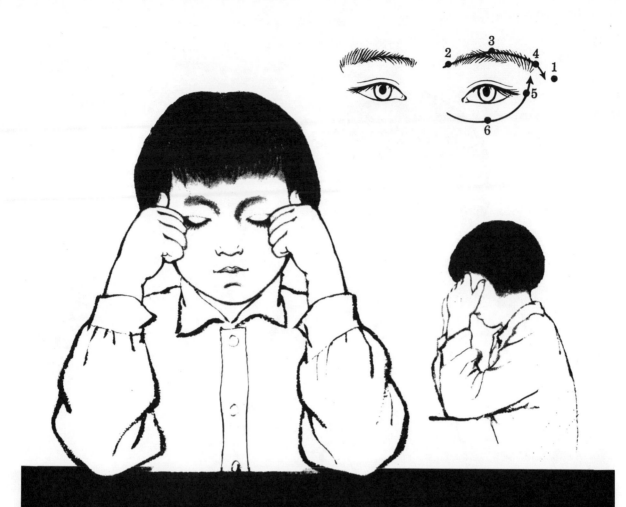

第四节　按太阳穴轮刮眼眶(太阳、拈竹、鱼腰、
丝竹空、瞳子髎、承泣等穴)

　　拳起四指,以左右大拇指罗纹面按太阳穴,
以左右食指第二节内侧面轮刮眼眶上下一圈,
先上后下,轮刮上下一圈计四拍。节拍8×8

FOURTH PART: PRESSING THE TAI YANG POINT AND STROKING AROUND THE EYE (1, TAI YANG: 2, ZHAN ZHU: 3, YU YAO: 4, SI ZHU KONG: 5, TONG ZI: 6, CHENG QI AND OTHER POINTS).

Curl the four fingers of each hand; use your thumbs to press your temples (the Tai Yang point). Following the numbered arrows above, bend your index fingers and use the flat part between the first and second joints to stroke in the upper half of a circle along your eyebrows, and then the lower half circle below your eyes creating a full circle. Always stroke from the inner corners of your eyes to the outer. Stroke each full circle to the count of four. Repeat sixteen times.

Chinese Embroidery Workers Exercises

The following exercises were described by a woman worker who guided an American group around an embroidery factory. The workers do the eye exercises twice a day.

Shut your eyes while you relax. Count to ten.

Stroke your eyebrows as you count to ten forward and backward.

Massage behind and in front of your ears, counting in the same manner.*

Sit erect and stare out into the distance for one or two minutes.

Try the Chinese routines several times as they are presented. Then pick the parts that seem to work best for you and repeat them regularly. Don't be afraid to deviate from the exercises as they are shown above. Apparently the Chinese vary the exercises to fit the different needs of factory workers and school children.

---

* We have no clear explanation of ear massage. Probably it stimulates nerve points, which are not always near the affected parts. It may also aid hearing.

Take Care of Your Eyes

Always try to be conscious of the work your eyes are doing, especially when you are reading for long periods or doing close work. Don't strain them until they sting and are bloodshot. When you are reading, rest them every page or two, if only for two or three seconds, and be sure to use bright comfortable lighting that illumines your whole work area.

Protect your eyes from dirt, smoke, foreign objects. Wear safety glasses that can't shatter and use goggles when working around materials that could fly into your eyes. Don't rub your eyes, especially when dirt gets into them. You can scratch the cornea, causing more pain and possible permanent damage. Take the same precautions if you wear contact lenses. Wash dirt out by blinking or with an eye bath. If the pain persists, if the foreign matter won't come out, or if your eye is punctured, see a doctor immediately.

Have your eyes checked regularly by an ophthalmologist especially if you think something is wrong.

Exercise your eyes to keep them in shape, just as you regularly exercise your whole body.

Daily Exercise Chart for Quick Reference

Relax. Contemplate. Breathe at a smooth, even pace throughout.

1. Focus on a point at a comfortable distance, concentrate on its clarity and then on seeing your total field of vision (one minute).
2. Palm your eyes (thirty seconds).
3. Swing your head from side to side and concentrate on the streaks of light (fifteen seconds). Swing your head up and down and concentrate on the vertical streaks (fifteen seconds).
4. Palm your eyes (thirty seconds).
5. Look straight up and down five times, slowly. Look from side to side five times, slowly. Look diagonally upper left to lower right five times, slowly. Look diagonally upper right to lower left five times, slowly.
6. Palm your eyes (thirty seconds).
7. Follow the upper edge of vision in an arch back and forth three times, slowly. Follow the lower edge of vision in an arch back and forth three times, slowly.
8. Follow a complete circle by rolling your eyes around the edges three times in each direction slowly.
9. Palm your eyes (thirty seconds, longer if necessary).
10. Follow your thumb with your focal point out and back five times, slowly.
11. Palm your eyes for one full minute or until they feel completely relaxed and unstrained.
12. Follow the Chinese massage exercise (fifteen minutes).

4 / The Eye, the Mind, and Meditation

A strong, healthy young man donates a pint of blood. Afterwards he sits at a table munching candy and cookies. He sees his peripheral vision start blacking out, fading away gradually toward his focal point. He feels a sensation like traveling down a tunnel, and then he passes out cold, slumping over on the table, mashing the cookies into scattered crumbs. A nurse rushes to his aid.

A drunk sees his world spinning endlessly, gets sick, and passes out.

A drug freak takes a good-sized dose of LSD and sees a whole new world— sometimes frightening, sometimes beyond his idea of beauty.

A hospital patient running a high fever sees his room draped in a strange yellow light.

A fasting mystic sees visions and feels closer to the Infinite.

A sleeping beauty sees her handsome prince as she dreams away the night.

These are just a few of the different kinds of extraordinary visual experiences that catch our imaginations. Everyone talks about them and feels curious about their meanings. Visions befuddle us.

We know that if things don't "look" right, something must be wrong. As doctors check us over, they search our eyes for changes in the retina and ask if our vision has altered. They know that our eyes are easily affected by illness. For instance, some types of mental illnesses change the way the individual sees, and these deviations help doctors diagnose a specific illness.

Our visual sense is an integral part of our total being that reacts to the environment as it is and to heightened perceptions of that reality.

Look and see! Dick, Jane, and Spot! From the beginnings of our education come memories of the importance of seeing.

Dick and Jane grow up with television, movies, magazines, billboards, and picture books. They are bombarded with visual material and are addicted to it. They need visual stimulation, but they have no idea why and have never stopped to appreciate what and how they see.

Our eyes are like swinging double doors to our brains. All the material that comes through can have profound effects on our emotions, thoughts, preferences, and prejudices. By learning to control our visual sense, we can control our inner tensions and develop a more balanced sense of well-being. We have that ability built in, but we must learn to find it and use it.

To that end, research into alpha-wave receivers and transmitters has recently introduced new meditation and hypnosis techniques. Special electronic equipment can pick up alpha-wave transmissions that the brain emits. The equipment then translates the impulses into audible sounds so you can learn to control your own production of alpha waves. Alpha waves have been found to be produced by various states of rest and meditation, and in many cases, eye exercises have been used to help achieve those states.

Eastern religions are well known for emphasizing the use of the physical body to achieve higher states of consciousness. The disciplines of Zen and yoga have become the most popular Eastern philosophies in the West, perhaps because they are tolerant of many different concepts of God and contain systems of mental and physical control that challenge our imagination. Both Zen and yoga recommend special eye exercises to help meditation. Zen masters meditate with open eyes, alert to surroundings; yogis meditate with eyes closed and seek visions of higher consciousness.*

Personally, I've always avoided the strictures of one discipline and have tended toward a mix-and-match approach. It's more important to feel a sense of visual openness, to control the eye-to-mind process, than it is to argue the merits of any one approach.

After a discussion of the potentials of the eye-to-mind process with a friend, she said, "It sounds like you are saying that improving your vision improves your visions." Well, if I could soft-pedal the mystical implications of the word *visions*, the statement is significant. Achieving control of the eye-to-mind process opens the mind to all sorts of possibilities, depending on how far you want to go. You are your own guide and you can determine your own path. If Zen and yoga help, use them. You'll find your eyes are one means to help you along the path.

---

* For an interesting series of studies on mental disciplines, see Charles T. Tart (ed.). *Altered States of Consciousness.* New York: Doubleday, 1972.

Preparations for Meditations

Read through all the material in this section. Then test the directions on yourself. Choose a regular routine. You may arrange a special time each day or you may decide to take a piecemeal approach, mixing and matching whatever exercises and meditations you wish. Any approach is better than none. I recommend five minutes of eye excercises followed by fifteen minutes of eye meditation.

As you proceed, first learn to relax your whole body including your eyes. You should be completely familiar with palming by now, and you should make use of it any time your eyes feel tired or strained. Palming becomes more effective the more you do it. You will find it helps you to wind down before starting the exercise. Even if you do nothing else, palming is a helpful aid to meditation. If you attempt all the exercises in this section in one session, be sure to palm your eyes for at least thirty seconds between exercises.

Adopt a receptive frame of mind. The attitude of the individual determines the quality of his experience.

Be nonchalant rather than serious and determined.

Be creative. The creative mind seeks new sensations and is open to the essential qualities of new experience.

Breathe. Try to concentrate on an established breathing pattern. Breathe deeply through your nose, pushing out your belly as you inhale. Hold a couple of seconds, then exhale slowly pulling in your belly. Hold a couple of seconds, and inhale. Don't breathe too heavily or too softly.

Contemplate deep within your physical self and then more deeply. Feel your own presence, your own existence. See yourself seeing.

Find a comfortable seated position.

Focus on one point about four or five feet out in front of you at eye level. Concentrate on seeing that point as clearly and intensely as you can.

This exercise is basically a repeat of the focal point exercise described earlier. It is included here because it helps relieve the mind of its tensions and preoccupations.

The mind itself has a focal ability capable of functioning in conjunction with any of your senses; it functions particularly well in partnership with your visual focal point. The mind's focus concentrates best on one item or idea at a time. So when you stop your eyes and focus on one point and really concentrate, you are giving your mind a specific focus. All other preoccupations blur out into peripheral areas of the mind, just as your eyes see peripheral objects less distinctly.

Hold your concentration on that focal point for as long as is comfortable. In time, you will develop the ability to hold your focus for extended periods.

Palm your eyes.

Open and close your eyes in a slow blink.

Stop, shut your eyes, and recall in your mind the image you saw when your eyes were momentarily open. Try to remember exactly what you saw most clearly as you reconstruct the picture in your mind's eye.

As soon as you have formed a complete image, blink your eyes again in another direction. Repeat the process about five times.

Artists, photographers, and other creative people find this kind of visualization helpful in developing the ability to recreate pictorial images clearly. It also helps improve memory and the ability to see rapidly changing events.

Squeeze your eyelids as tightly shut as possible.

Relax the tension.

Palm your eyes. Concentrate on the blackness.

Rest.

Inside Looking Out

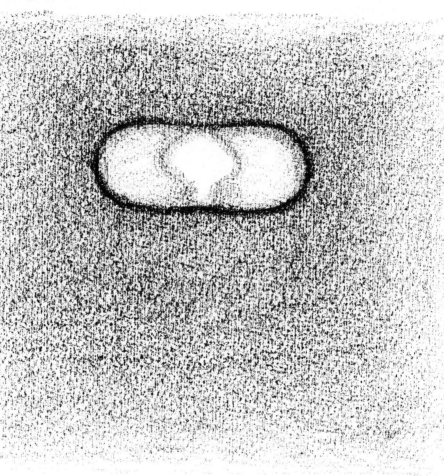

Sit in a comfortable position and concentrate.

Pull your consciousness back inside yourself as you look out through your eyes.

Imagine your visual field shrinking smaller and smaller as you concentrate more and more on your inner self.

Close your eyes.

Meditate on the inner sights and sounds, the afterimages, and the vibrations of your breathing.

Nothingness

With your eyes open, contemplate the absence of an ability to perceive light.

Out beyond your frame of seeing, you perceive nothing.

Not blackness.

Nothingness.

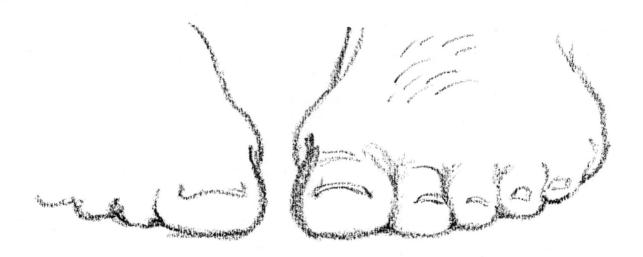

Toes have the ability to see nothingness.

They feel, but see nothing.

Comprehending Nothingness

·

Cover your left eye and hold this page approximately twelve inches from your right eye. Focus on the small dot.

As you hold your focus on the dot, move the page slowly toward your eye, then away. Stop in different positions until the scribble in the periphery becomes invisible. For this to work, it is important that you keep your focus on the small dot.

To repeat the exercise with the left eye, turn the book upside down.

At the junction of the optic nerve with the retina of the eye, there is no light-perceiving ability. Therefore, the eye perceives nothing.

If you follow this exercise properly, the scribble on the right will fall on that junction and disappear—a good example of the lack of light perception built into the eyeball.

Again, cover the left eye, hold the page approximately twelve inches from your right eye, and focus on the dot on the left.

As before, the white spot within the stripes can be made to disappear.

The field of lines appears continuous, uninterrupted.

The white spot appears to become nothingness, exerting no effect on its surrounding field.

Without the ability of the eye to read past the junction of the optic nerve with the retina, you would see two pronounced spots within your visual field, one for each eye.

Turn the page upside down to repeat the exercise with the other eye.

Now, again contemplate nothingness.

Palm your eyes.

Light Saturation

Find a place with bright illumination. If you can't be in the sunlight, look out a window. If you don't have a window, a brightly lit room will do.

Concentrate on holding still in a seated position. Focus on a point straight ahead of you. As you hold this position, your eyes may begin to sting, so blink your eyelids when necessary, but not too often.

Breathe slowly and smoothly. Hold this position for three minutes.

After a minute or two your retina will begin to become saturated with light. The effect is similiar to that of the afterimage, but on a larger scale. More of the retina is involved. Light areas may become mysteriously brighter, change color, spill over into dark areas, or pulsate. Objects may appear to have halos around them.

After three minutes or so, close your eyes and imagine the scene you just saw. Keep your head straight and still.

Hold this position for twenty seconds or so, then open your eyes and focus directly on the spot you were concentrating on.

Colors and lights change. Different effects occur in different settings, varying with different states of mind and with different patterns of breathing. If you are in a receptive frame of mind, you can experience and discover visions of your own. Don't strain and never stare directly into the sun.

After a few minutes rest your eyes by palming.

Yoga Gazing Exercises (Thratakam)

Yoga eye concentration exercises help to establish a state of meditation as well as strengthen the eyes.

In a seated position, place a lighted candle with the flame at your eye level about three or four feet from your body. Actually, any small spot that you can focus on will work, but the candle flame is best.

Gaze at the flame for a minute without blinking.

Close your eyelids, relax, and imagine the flame to be behind the area between your eyebrows for a minute.

Stare at the flame again and close your eyes, repeating this cycle for a total of five or six minutes. Over a long period of time you can gradually work up to holding the gaze for three minutes and closing the eyes for three minutes.

There are more advanced gazing exercises that involve extended staring at the tip of the nose and gazing at an imagined area, the third eye, said to be inside the head between the eyebrows. These are the most strenuous eye exercises I have found, and they should only be attempted, at length, under the supervision of a good yoga instructor.*

---

* See Swami Vishnudevananda. *The Complete Illustrated Book of Yoga.* New York: Bell, 1960. Yogiraj Sri Swami Satchidananda. *Integral Yoga Hatha.* New York: Holt, 1970.

Developing Creative Skills

Close your eyes and try to imagine your present environment with as many details as possible. Try to imagine a drawing, painting, or photograph that you like. Try to imagine a clear picture of a past or future environment or a picture of someone you love.

This is visualization—your ability to form mental pictures.

You are a visionary. If you can find a means to communicate your personal vision, you are an artist.

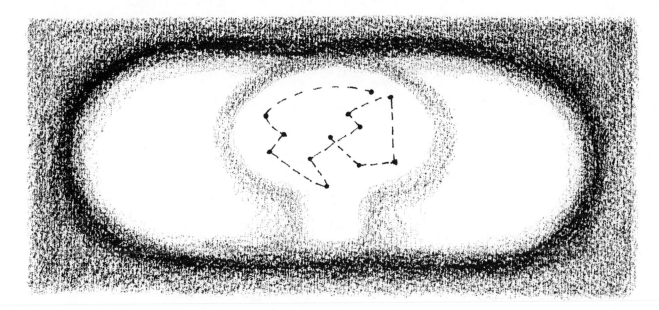

Mix up exercises you like.

Dance with your eyes. Jump your focal point from one point of interest to another. Ask yourself why you stopped at a particular point.

Your eyes will prefer some points over others, telling you something about your subliminal likes and dislikes.

Consciously moving your focal point around your environment exercises your focal ability and helps you to explore your environment more thoroughly.

Eye Massage

Palm your eyes and relax with your eyes closed.

Press your fingertips firmly to the area between your eyebrows.

Make a circular motion, rubbing gently but firmly for about ten seconds. Then begin moving your hands apart and slowly massage your eyebrows, temples, cheeks, sides of the nose, and back again to the area between your eyebrows.

Take as much time as you feel you need. Repeat as needed.

Don't rub the eyeball itself.

Palm your eyes for thirty seconds after the massage.

The Chinese exercises discussed previously are also recommended at this point.

You will find that the massage is instantly relaxing. It clears up minor tension headaches, relieves eyestrain, and has the added effect of stimulating the skin and controlling wrinkles.

Don't press your eyeballs directly. The pressure can throw your eyes out of focus for hours. Blinking and eye movement exercises are all you need for eyeball massage.

New Points of View

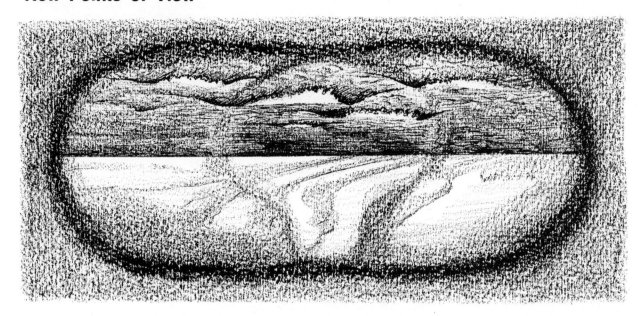

Change your visual orientation to the world.

Stand on your head, or with your head on the floor look out from between your legs.

Hold your head sideways.

Wear a blindfold for an hour or more.

Wear a patch over one eye.

Make drawings of your individual perceptions.

Personalized Seeing

To make the most of these experiences, you must personalize the process—choose the exercises that you like, that make you feel good, that give you creative ideas, that expand your consciousness. Practice those exercises in any order you find helpful, or make up your own exercises, but always remember to relax and rest your eyes any time you feel tension or strain. Even if you try only a few, your eye-to-mind process will have been opened at least for a moment. You have a start. You will feel your own presence and worth. And richer experience is on the way.

Seeing myself see has been an important part of my work as an artist. I have been concerned with capturing some of the internal qualities of seeing. I have frozen my focal point at one point for hours to make drawings and paintings of my whole field of perception. I have devised panoramic paintings that curve around the eyes and have studied hundreds of visual effects. The possibilities seem endless.

In the introduction to this book I describe how I began to see the process and how it excited me. I believe those experiences are available to everyone. It's just a matter of turning inward. Nothing special. Just seeing a part of nature that we overlook—ourselves.

An artist usually wants to lead other people into the experiences he has had, to cause them to feel as he does, to share his experience and not just possess it for himself. For me there has been something creative and calming about being able actually to see how my eyes function and to learn how that function affects what I see. This internal visual awareness seems just as important as looking at an object and appreciating its beauty. The search for beauty is good, but not better than the search for self-awareness.

Seeing yourself see is the most basic visual experience. It's always with you. You are standing inside yourself, seeing yourself standing there.

5 / Art and Visual Apperception

Drawing Exercise

Get some big sheets of paper and a pencil and draw. It's the best way to begin to understand what creative seeing is about. And it's a good way to understand the possible benefits of visual self-awareness—visual apperception.

Place yourself in front of a large sheet of paper (at least thirty inches wide), which can be on an easel, a desk, or the floor.

Make a dot in the middle of the sheet. Let that dot represent your focal point.

Look directly ahead at your surroundings over the top of the sheet of paper. You don't have to bother with any kind of still-life setup.

Fix your focal point on any convenient point that happens to be directly in line with your position, and place your pencil on the dot in the middle of the paper.

As you stare at the focal point, try to draw all the major parts of your surroundings. Don't look at the paper or move your focal point from its position.

Try to let the whole sheet represent your total field of vision.

If you don't see things clearly, don't try to draw them clearly. Just let a scribble or smudge represent the vague forms you see out in the periphery of your field of vision.

When you draw an object, you are usually only concerned with that object and not with the space and shapes around it that make up the total environment. Of course, locking your focal point in one position and trying to draw won't help you make a realistic drawing, but it will help you capture some of the aspects of your total field of vision. Your visual sensibilities are expanded so that you are more open to the creative possibilities of your own personal way of seeing.

THIS DRAWING WAS CREATED BY A NINTH-GRADE STUDENT, RICHARD DUNBAR, AGED 14, IN RESPONSE TO THE PRECEDING EXERCISE.

Use another large sheet of paper set up in the same way. This time as you draw, look at the paper and move your focal point around freely, but keep your head straight so that your total field of vision doesn't change.

Try to make the whole sheet represent your total field of vision.

Draw details as you desire, but pay special attention to the areas your focal point automatically falls on.

108

Notice that the objects that appear large at first glance are actually very small when seen in proportion to your total scope of vision. Also notice that it is necessary to distort the drawing if it is to show the curved field of vision on a flat sheet of paper.

I've assigned these exercises to a wide range of students in my experience as a teacher, and I've always elicited a reaction. The students have always responded at first with disbelief and apprehension. Gradually they become excited as they begin seeing and drawing. They surprise themselves and often laugh at the results, and this helps to dilute the fear of failing to make a "perfect" picture. Sometimes they ridicule the idea, suggesting that all my talk about the eyes belongs in a science class. But they understand, and it shows as their work progresses.

RICHARD'S RESPONSE TO THE SECOND EXERCISE.

Sensory Feedback

Art is illusive. An artist's intentions are even more illusive. His desire to convey some of the qualities of his own seeing is a personal struggle often overlooked. Part of being an artist is wanting to communicate your personal vision of the world. A few artists (like Cézanne and Monet) realize that there is a difference between their envisioned world and the world perceived by the eye, and those few attempt to make their visual apperceptions a vital element of their work. Their art recreates visual stimulations and effects their experience both consciously and subconsciously. I believe we are mysteriously drawn to art that reiterates our own subliminal sensory structures just as we tend to be drawn to music that beats the rhythm of our hearts.

The eyes not only send the brain messages to be translated into images, they send those messages, or nerve impulses, within a structure that the eyes have built into themselves. The nature of that structure has an effect on the pictures the brain forms. The structures of the TV camera and the picture tube predetermine that the image on the TV screen will be a certain shape and that it will be made up of horizontal lines. We are seldom aware of those lines or of the shape of the tube because we are much more interested in what is happening in the picture. If we want to know the total effect of television or any other visual medium, we must know the inherent effect of the structure as well as the effect of the information it conveys.

If an artist creates a painting that has a point directly in the middle that seems to be more sharply defined than the other areas, or if he paints on a large scale so that the painting seems to create an environment of its own by taking in most of the field of vision, he is either consciously or unconsciously attempting to create a feedback effect. The central point of the painting, quite subliminally, reiterates the focal point within the field of vision. The large canvas echoes the broad sweep of vision, and the visual perception mechanisms in the eye and the brain respond with curiosity to this feedback.

Better sensory training would enrich the creative potential of all of us. We cannot truly create original concepts of art and science without experience, and all experience passes through our senses on its way to the reasoning centers of our brains. So it seems only logical to give those senses more attention.

The tantra paintings of the Eastern religious tradition rely on the ability of the meditating artist to search deep within himself and his perception. As he paints in a continuous state of meditation, he develops a composition that has a symmetrical structure that can be closely related to the visual field. In fact, the very symmetry of the field of vision may account for the constant recurrence of symmetrical compositions in art and architecture throughout history in all cultures. Zen painting works in another direction that focuses on the perception of the real world rather than the mystical inner visions of tantra. The Zen artist learns about his sense structures thoroughly and then composes work that serves as a counterpoint to the symmetry of vision. He intentionally works off-center and emphasizes voids; yet he achieves a feeling for the presence of himself seeing.

Painters East and West try to sharpen their visual senses and develop close coordination between eye and hand. There's nothing especially mystical about this. The musician sharpens his hearing; the dancer his sense of touch, balance, and movement; the gourmet chef his sense of taste and smell. The architect and today's mixed-media artist attempt interactions among two or more of the senses. Of course, the amount of attention any one individual artist gives to his experienced sensations varies. Some work from a purely intuitive base and some, like Leonardo da Vinci, study in such depth that they make important contributions outside the arts and in the sciences. In turn, scientists who study the senses make important discoveries that the artist eagerly employs.

Perspective

The ancient Greeks tried to understand the physical aspects of the response of the viewer; they adjusted architecture and statues to account for the vantage point of the viewer. Statues mounted high on a building were sculpted with slightly enlarged heads and shoulders so that the viewer saw an apparently properly proportioned figure. Heroes and gods looked grand rather than pinheaded. The Greeks also noticed that the more distant an object was, the smaller it appeared to the eye, so they occasionally applied this idea to mural paintings. That was the first suggestion of perspective.

The concern for creating the illusion of reality led Renaissance artists to analyze how their eyes perceived the world. It wasn't a problem of copying reality, but of creating an object of art that convinced the viewer that what he was seeing was real whether it actually existed or not. The search led to the development of our present system of perspective, which depicts the physical vantage point of the artist in such a way as to convince the viewer that he is standing in the artist's shoes. The Renaissance was infatuated with perspective, not just in painting but in architecture and theater. The proscenium arch theater, the basic design of our present day theaters and movie houses, was primarily an outgrowth of this infatuation. Stages were designed as enormous framed pictures with lines of perspective that receded up a stage that tilted steeply down toward the audience. Lines of perspective converged at a point on a painted horizon line at the rear center of the stage. All sets were carefully designed to appear to diminish into the distance. The effect worked best for the viewer with a good seat directly in the middle of the theater at a height equal to the vanishing point at the back of the set. Of course, those seats were reserved for dignitaries; the rest of the audience had to make do with a strangely distorted view of a slanted stage with sets that looked as if they might slide into the front rows.

BAROQUE PAINTERS MADE THE MOST OF AERIAL PERSPECTIVE IN THEIR ELABORATE CEILING MURALS. Giovanni Battista Tiepolo, *Aurora Dispersing the Clouds of Night: Ceiling from the Mocenigo Palace, Venice.* Venetian 1696–1770. Canvas 72″ × 54″. Purchased, Maria Antoinette Evans Fund. 30.539. Courtesy Museum of Fine Arts, Boston.

The elaborate rules of perspective were extended to every situation. Baroque and rococo painters exaggerated the effects of perspective with complex compositions of objects receding farther and farther into the distance. To capitalize on the effect, they placed heavy frames of ornate three-dimensional carving around their pictures, so that the viewer's eye might be fooled into believing the illusion. Sometimes it works very effectively. You see the objects on the frame sticking out into the room and then those same objects are painted into the picture so convincingly that you feel the surface of the painting has become a hole in the wall. This technique was especially successful on ceiling paintings because it is easier to fool the eye with unfamiliar points of view—most of us don't look up and see angels floating in the clouds. In the better attempts, the ceiling seems to have been removed by the artist so that you too can look up and believe that you see floating angels, at least for a moment.

The Panorama (or Diorama)

Nineteenth century natural history museums devised the panorama, a painting that curves around the viewer to give him a feeling of being surrounded by a landscape. As you look around, the landscape actually does seem to curve, partly because the turning action is curved, but primarily because your peripheral perception takes in an image that is actually curved by the position of the eyes on the head and by the curvature of the retina. The effect of the panorama is well used to depict the total environment of a particular subject. Stuffed specimens, rocks, trees, and soil are arranged in front of the curved painting. Properly done, it is extremely realistic. The panorama effect has also been employed in the movies; in the 1950s the Cinerama movie corporation built special screens that actually curved around the front of the audience. It took three projectors in perfect synchronization to cover the screen, and when they worked well the effect was overwhelming. The audience screamed as the film zoomed them down steep rollercoaster rides. Unfortunately, the mechanics were too expensive and complex to survive. Supersized 70-mm film shot with wide-angle lens and projected on a large flat screen took over, but never achieved the same sensations. Disappointingly, a recent release of *This Is Cinerama* was transferred to 70-mm film, and lacked the effect of the original three-projector version.

Impressionism

The nineteenth century also produced a new kind of perceptual interest among painters. The Impressionists were tired of the academic approach to reality. They weren't interested in the elaborate rules of perspective or the established procedures of academic painting. They moved directly out into the landscape and let nature play on their senses. From those sensations, they painted canvases quickly so as not to lose the vitality of the moment. They studied how light made the facets of nature glisten and how light activated their eyes in particular situations. The varieties of light created

NATURAL HISTORY MUSEUMS USE CURVED PAINTINGS AT THE REAR OF PANORAMAS TO SIMULATE THE VISUAL EFFECT CREATED BY THE TURNING OF THE EYES AND BY THE CURVATURE OF THE RETINA. THE PAINTED HORIZON CURVES JUST AS IT WOULD APPEAR IN THE ACTUAL SETTING. Lake Dwellers diorama courtesy of The Museum of Science, Boston, Massachusetts.

WIDE-SCREEN MOVIES EVOLVED TO TAKE IN PERIPHERAL VISION. NOTICE THAT THE HEIGHT AND THE WIDTH ARE ROUGHLY THE SAME PROPORTION AS THE FIELD OF VISION, AND IN THIS PARTICULAR SHOT THE COMPOSITION ECHOES THE VISUAL FRAMEWORK. Scene from Stanley Kubrick's *2001: A Space Odyssey.* Courtesy The Museum of Modern Art/Film Stills Archive.

moments when objects and colors blended, and moments when everything took on a colored monotone.

Cézanne was engrossed by the way three-dimensional forms and spaces were seen by his eyes. He discovered that forms and spaces could be ambiguous, sometimes appearing to advance and recede simultaneously. He studied the way the focal point was able to reach out and "touch" the shape of forms and the way it jumped from one point of interest to another in any particular situation. His brush strokes are like the accumulation of those points, adding up to forms defined by color and revealed by light.

Influenced by new scientific theories about the nature of color perception, Seurat developed a pointillistic style by placing small dots of pure color side by side to create tones that were optically blended. Painters were beginning to paint visual sensations at the sacrifice of subject matter and were critically attacked for just that, as if they might bring on a new age of hedonism.

The Impressionists were just as impressed with patterns of light that occurred within the peripheral areas of vision as earlier artists had been impressed with the illusions of perspective. Monet applied a kind of spontaneous response to his visual sensations when he painted the *Water Lilies* late in his career. The giant canvases in the Museum of Modern Art in New York show large movements of light that are out of focus on the outer edges, but become more detailed as they move toward the central area. This format evolves directly from attempts at capturing a momentary effect on the total field of vision. A large three-part painting is even hung so that the two side panels surround the viewer, creating a sensation of walking into a new environment of radiant color.

A LARGE THREE-PART PAINTING OF MONET'S IS HUNG SO THAT THE TWO SIDE PANELS SURROUND THE VIEWER, CREATING THE SENSATION OF WALKING INTO A WORLD OF SPLASHING COLOR. Claude Monet, *Water Lilies* (c. 1920). Oil on canvas, triptych, each section, 6'6" × 14'. Collection, The Museum of Modern Art, New York. Mrs. Simon Guggenheim Fund.

It is possible that Monet became more concerned with the significance of his visual sensations when he began losing his sight in 1900, just as we all become conscious of the value of our senses when they begin to fail. An operation only slightly improved his vision, but he still painted, possibly trying to capture the blurred and indistinct effects his failing eyes perceived. His creative genius flowered in tragedy; where another painter might have given up art entirely, Monet accommodated to his handicap. He painted on a large scale, using sweeping gestures that enabled him to see what he was doing and let the viewer in on the excitement of his new perceptions at the same time.

Cubism

The Cubists followed in the tailstream of the Impressionists, realizing that vision could have a multiple purpose. With an emphasis on the form of things, they used the focal point and its movement to "touch" objects at a distance, as Cézanne had done, and to present different angles of view on one surface produced by an actively inquiring focal point. Braque and Picasso reiterated the oval shape of the central visual field by painting occasionally in an oval format. They imitated the central focus of vision by painting the middle of their compositions with clear edges and interesting details, while they let the outer edges fade into simple planes of muted colors. The viewer's own focal point is allowed to pick and choose details of its own liking, and there were some rather bizarre details to choose from.

Giacometti was a post-Cubist sculptor and painter who worked through a real sense of the value of the human eye and its influence on our lives. I quote Peter Selz, from the introduction to the Museum of Modern Art catalogue, *Alberto Giacometti*, 1965:

"He strives to discover the visual appearance and to render it with precision —not the reflections of light which occupied the Impressionists, nor the distorted view of the camera which fails to register distance, but the object as it is contained in space, as seen by the human eye, the artist's eye. . . .

"He explained that he could really not see me as I sat next to him—I was a conglomeration of vague and disconnected details—but that each member of the family sitting across the room was clearly visible, though diminutive, thin surrounded by enormous slices of space."

Le Corbusier, architect and painter, suggested that the rectangular drawing papers most commonly available are produced in those elongated proportions because they harmonize with the field of vision. He also felt that the horizontal nature of that field made horizontal paintings more pleasing than vertical ones. Many of the Cubists relied on theories of this sort to make art that had a close kinship to built-in structures of human perception.

CUBISTS OFTEN REITERATED THE OVAL SHAPE OF THE VISUAL FIELD WITH ITS CENTRAL AREA OF FOCUS. Georges Braque, *Still Life with Dice and Pipe,* 1911. Oil, 31½″ × 23″ (oval).

GIACOMETTI'S INTENSE CONCERN FOR RENDERING THE WAY HIS EYES DID THEIR
SEEING LED HIM TO WORK FEVERISHLY TOWARD CAPTURING THE IMPRESSION OF
A CENTRAL FOCUS SURROUNDED BY LARGE AREAS OF LIVING SPACE. Alberto Gia-
cometti, *The Artist's Mother*. 1950. Oil on canvas, 35⅜" × 24". Collection, The Museum of
Modern Art, New York. Acquired through the Lillie P. Bliss Bequest.

Current Art

Present-day artists are often concerned with the phenomenon of seeing. Josef Albers has developed the most comprehensive artist's color theory to date by detailed study of the interrelation of color and its effect on the eyes.

Op artists rely on the effects of afterimages and optical illusions to create vibrating lines, colors, and surfaces.

Psychedelic artists use drugs to stimulate visual hallucinations, which they then try to paint in a way that might possibly induce a high in the viewer.

Contemporary mandala painters try to work in well-disciplined states of meditation that help them to visualize mystical and spiritual images.

Color-field painters and abstract expressionists paint as large as possible in order to cover as much of the field of vision as possible.

Modern painting composition is strongly based on visual phenomena and can often be defined as relating the artist's particular concept to the field of vision.

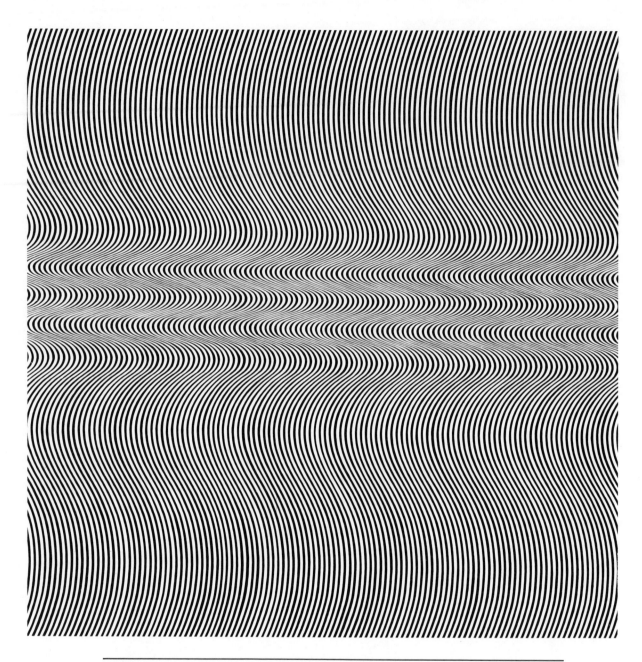

CONTEMPORARY ARTISTS OFTEN EMPLOY ILLUSORY EFFECTS THAT DIRECTLY CON-
FRONT THE VIEWER'S EYES. SOMETIMES THEY RAISE PERPLEXING PERCEPTUAL
QUESTIONS THAT HAVE NOT BEEN SUCCESSFULLY EXPLAINED BY SCIENCE. Bridget
Riley, *Current*. 1964. Synthetic polymer paint on composition board, 58⅜″ × 58⅞″. Col-
lection, The Museum of Modern Art, New York. Philip Johnson Fund.

HERE IS AN EXAMPLE OF MY OWN EFFORT, A CURVED PAINTING INSPIRED BY THE SURROUNDING SWEEP OF A FOGGY DAY NEAR THE WATER. Jim Jackson, *Water and Fog.* 1971. 24″ × 48″.

Conclusion

Hopefully your struggles with the exercises and ideas in this book have enlarged your understanding of the function of your eyes and the role they play in your life. But this is only a beginning. The total flowering of understanding can only come from personal experience. You've made a start, and that is the hardest part. The next step is to apply that essential motivation to the effort of turning your curiosity into creative expression. But don't belittle your efforts even if they seem to go nowhere at first. Your approach and insights are as valid as those of any artist, guru, mystic, or saint. They all struggled when they started too. Seeing yourself see can help you to establish self-confidence and a sense of validity. Even if you have no desire to draw or paint, visual apperception helps affirm the vitality of your existence.

It is as simple as the focal point concentration exercise. You can't be conscious of your focal point without being conscious of the total field of vision which, in turn, grows into a consciousness of your whole being—existing. This reassured frame of mind is the foundation for the development of an open-minded sense of aesthetics that works without being told to follow a set of rules that may have been devised out of someone else's prejudiced opinion of what beauty is.

Human evolution has brought us to a point where we can understand ourselves better than ever before. Still, there is a long way to go and a lot of potential that needs to be explored in the expansion of our minds. R. D. Laing, the popular psychologist, recently spoke of how he had learned to open up to the excitement of seeing, to move his eyes all around to improve his sense of self, and he suggested that everyone could benefit from similar experience. That has been my purpose in writing this book.

Our world is not just seen. It is heard, smelled, felt, balanced, tasted, touched, cooled, weighted, etc. Sensory education puts us in touch with the give and take, the action and reaction alliance with our world. It points out our vital need for a healthy environment as well as a healthy mind and body. Sensory education teaches us to experience our senses consciously; it teaches us how to care for and improve their function and to appreciate fully their significance and use. We could use more of it in our schools. Why not start with something like the Chinese approach to visual care?

You can know your vision, and use that knowledge to form a give-and-take relationship with all that you experience, materially and spiritually. Your eyes can be tools for creative accomplishment. Artists and musicians are among the few who make the most of their senses, but there is no reason why anyone else can't find a way to apply creative skills through the development of all his senses. Make your whole life an art form. Tune in to your total being. Hear yourself hearing. See yourself seeing.

"Maintain the unity of your will. Do not listen with ears, but with the mind.

Do not listen with the mind, but with the spirit. The function of the ear ends with the hearing; that of the mind with symbols or ideas. But the spirit is an emptiness ready to receive all things."*

Ditto for seeing.

---

* Chapter XII, *Chuang Tzu.* Quoted from Mai-mai Sze, "Zen and the Arts." From Nancy Wilson Ross. *The World of Zen.* New York: Random House, 1960.

Bibliography

Albers, Josef. *Interaction of Color*. New Haven: Yale Univ. Press, 1971.

Bates, W. H. *Better Eyesight Without Glasses*. New York: Holt, 1940.

Cogniat, Raymond. *Monet and His World*. New York: Viking, 1966.

Corbett, Margaret Darst. *Help Yourself to Better Sight*. No. Hollywood, Calif.: Wilshire, 1949.

Giacometti, Alberto. *Alberto Giacometti*. Introduction by Peter Selz. New York: Museum of Modern Art, 1965. Distributed by Doubleday.

Gibson, James J. *The Perception of the Visual World*. Boston: Houghton Mifflin, 1950.

Gombrich, E. H. *Art and Illusion*. New York: Pantheon Books, 1960.

Gregory, R. L. *Eye and Brain*. New York: World Univ. Library, 1966.

Herbert, R. L. *Modern Artists on Art*. Englewood Cliffs, N.J.: Prentice-Hall, 1964.

Huxley, Aldous. *The Art of Seeing*. New York: Harper & Row, 1942.

Huxley, Aldous. *The Doors of Perception and Heaven and Hell*. New York: Harper & Row, 1954.

Kahnweiler, Daniel-Henry. *The Rise of Cubism*. Translated by Henry Aronson. New York: Wittenborn Schultz, 1949.

Kraskin, Robert A. *How To Improve Your Vision*. No. Hollywood, Calif.: Wilshire, 1973.

Payne, Buryl. *Getting There Without Drugs*. New York: Viking, 1973.

Rewald, John. *Paul Cezanne Letters*. Translated by Marguerite Rey. Oxford: Cassover, 1946.

Rosanes-Berrett, Marilyn B. *Do You Really Need Eyeglasses?* New York: Hart, 1974.

Ross, Nancy Wilson. *The World of Zen: An East-West Anthology*. New York: Random House, 1960.

Satchidananda, Yogiraj Sri Swami. *Integral Yoga Hatha*. New York: Holt, 1970.

Science for the People. *China: Science Walks on Two Legs*. New York: Avon, 1974.

Stearn, Jesse. *Yoga, Youth and Reincarnation*. New York: Bantam Books, 1965.

Tart, Charles T. (ed.). *Altered States of Consciousness*. New York: Doubleday, 1972.

Vishnudevananda, Swami. *The Complete Illustrated Book of Yoga*. New York: Bell, 1960.

Watson, Lyall. *Super Nature*. New York: Doubleday, 1973.

Wilentz, Joan Steen. *The Senses of Man*. New York: Crowell, 1968.